Is Anybody Up There?

Plus Healing Testimonies
and Inspirational Sermons

Dr. Loretta Blasingame

Loretta Blasingame Publishers

Unless otherwise indicated, all Scripture quotations are taken from the King James Version [KJV] of the *Bible,* 1611, public domain.

Is Anybody Up There?
Plus Healing Testimonies
and Inspirational Sermons

ISBN number 0-9787665-1-2
ISBN number 978-0-9787665-1-1

Published by:
Loretta Blasingame Publishers
P.O. Box 4058 Fullerton, CA 92834-4058

Printed in the United States of America.

Is Anybody Up There?

Dedication

This book is dedicated to my only child
Rickey Lee Blasingame, who was promoted
to Heaven on February 19, 1991.

He was the love of my life, my prayer partner,
and closest friend. For twenty-four years,
he made my day by serving God and loving both of us.

Rickey Lee Blasingame
1966 – 1991

Evelyn Roberts

Dear Loretta:

I've just finished your book. You have a remarkable testimony - much like others I've heard. I know Heaven must be much more wonderful than I can imagine. All those who have seen it describe it as unlike anything on the earth.

Praise the Lord, I get to go there some day.

I enjoyed the testimonies of healings in your book. I think they help to build faith in those who have needs.

The places you mentioned our ministry are as factual as I can remember. I'm sure many things happened that we don't even know about. You're welcome to use them just as they are.

God bless this book and make it a blessing to many.

Sincerely

Evelyn Roberts

Letter from Evelyn Roberts, Wife of Dr. Oral Roberts

INTRODUCTION - COMMENTS FROM

SIR LIONEL LUCKHOO

God has called all mankind to service, and His expectations for us are set out in the Word. As His children, we are blessed in a measure, but to some he has endowed superlative gifts. Loretta Blasingame is one of His children who has been especially gifted. Her grace emanates from an out of body experience, when Almighty God revived her from death and sent her back to earth to resume her life here, and to minister to the hurt and sick, and to comfort and heal those in distress.

I have traveled in the crusades, both in and out of America with Evangelist Loretta, and I have witnessed incredible healings even without the laying on of hands whilst this blessed handmaiden preached Jesus.

The story of Evangelist Loretta Blasingame written herein should be read by ALL, believers and unbelievers. I know that by the reading of these pages God will use this book to bring miracles into their lives. God bless Loretta and her work.

Sir Lionel Luckhoo, "World's most successful criminal attorney", is listed in the "Guiness Book of World Records." He and Loretta Blasingame traveled in the U.S. and abroad where he held meetings for attorneys and Loretta held healing crusades. Sir Lionel Luckhoo, Worldwide Evangelist, was honored four times by Queen Elizabeth II, and was Ambassador for two nations simultaneously.

THE PURPOSE OF THIS BOOK

Acts 20:24

But none of these things move me, nor do I count my life dear to myself, so that I may finish my race with joy, and the ministry, which I received from the Lord Jesus, to testify to the gospel of the grace of God.

THE PURPOSE OF THIS MINISTRY

St. Luke 5:31-32

Jesus answered and said to them, those who are well have no need of a physician, but those who are sick. I have not come to call the righteous, but sinners, to repentance.

Special Acknowledgements

Thank you Paul and Jan Crouch, founders of Trinity Broadcasting Network (TBN), and Marcus and Joni Lamb, founders of Daystar Television Network.

You have opened the airways for my ministry to deliver testimonies of healing; messages of faith; sharing my heaven experience; and the privilege to pray for your television audience for healing.

God Bless you Paul and Jan, and Marcus and Joni for your great work through television for the Kingdom of God.

Yvonne Nance, Contributing Editor

Managing Editor of Oral Roberts

Editorial Department and Publications

for 25 years

CONTENTS

Part One - Is Anybody Up There?

Part Two - Miracles of Healing and Deliverance

Part Two Continued...

Part Three - My Favorite Sermons and Devotions

PART ONE

Is Anybody Up There?

Is Anybody Up There?

1

IS ANYBODY UP THERE?

I'll never forget the day I stood in the fields staring heavenward with an almost overwhelming yearning to know – there was something so mysterious about that sky and those clouds. I hungered to know what it was. I had my favorite spot in the field where I went every day to look up.

One day, with unfulfilled wonderment in my innocent blue eyes, I was searching the heavens. In an instant I called out:

"IS ANYBODY UP THERE?"

Suddenly, the fields were mysteriously quiet and strangely still. Even the livestock stood quiet and motionless. Then to my utter amazement, the silence was broken with a voice I had never heard. A revelation flashed across my heart and literally shook my entire being. I clearly heard a voice say: "I AM GOD…I AM HERE!"

To this day I have no idea how long I stood there frozen in that moment.

I never told a living soul, but every day after that I rushed out to the field to "my spot" to look up at the sky and talk to God.

I told Him all my problems; how hard life was for us in Arkansas; and how I wanted to move to the big city of Dallas, Texas.

Some of my older brothers and a sister had married and moved to Dallas. Their letters made Dallas sound like heaven.

Often, I secretly cried myself to sleep because I hated watching my mother working so hard to care for the family and the farm. I felt life in the city would be much easier on me, my mother and the family.

But God wasn't quite ready for us to leave Arkansas just yet. Way down deep inside my four-year-old mind, I knew this would not be my last encounter with such a Great and Glorious God.

2

MY UNSCHEDULED ARRIVAL IN HEAVEN

"I'm dead!" I thought as I saw my spirit rise out of my body. And yet, I could see and recognize everything in the room. Then up through the ceiling and away through the clouds, my spirit traveled through layers of brilliant, white clouds. The clouds looked like a million rows of giant cotton balls, floating on top of each other.

My physical body lay on the sterile, white-draped table in the doctor's office where I had collapsed from two simultaneous heart attacks. I was dead!

That summer morning in the 1960's, I was in my car driving the Dallas freeways, rushing as usual to take care of things that a busy young mother's schedule demands. Without warning, a pain struck my chest like a knife. I gripped the steering wheel, desperately trying to remain conscious while the pain ripped through my chest. Weak and frightened, I somehow managed to drive to my doctor's office in this agonizing pain.

Lying on the gurney in the emergency room, I was very sick. My muscles drew up until my fingers crossed over each other. The pain was almost unbearable. My chest felt like it was on fire. I became nauseated and overwhelmed with fear. As the doctor worked frantically over me, I heard him say: "She's had a heart attack! Has anyone called her husband?"

I thought, "*This is not the way I want to die!*"

Then I heard the doctor say, "Oh my God, she's gone!"

During the next ten minutes, I went to heaven.

I literally saw myself come out of my body and begin to rise. My spirit traveled through the office ceiling and then into the billowy white clouds.

Soon, I was seeing the most magnificent sight one could imagine. I saw myself arrive in heaven before two beautiful, huge gates. They swung open to admit me.

The beauty of these gates is indescribable. I saw emeralds, pearls, opals and diamonds. They sparkled with large precious gems. Some I had never seen. I entered the Gates of Glory, and saw a golden bridge before me, sparkling like crystal.

Then I saw Him, my beloved Jesus! The King of Kings and Lord of Lords! Jesus, Name above all Names! About six feet tall, Jesus was more glorious than I had ever imagined.

His beautiful hair was medium brown and waved to the top of His broad, divine shoulders. Every hair lay perfectly in place. His skin was firm, yet, soft and smooth.

His garment, "The Robe of Righteousness," was unbelievably white, glistening without spot or wrinkle. I beheld His beautiful, gloriously radiant face. I was overwhelmed by His Majesty.

He stretched out His arms toward me in a beckoning gesture and said simply – "Come."

Along the way, I saw kingdoms. I said to myself, "*I'm standing on top of many, many kingdoms!*"

All the buildings were built on top of each other like New York skyscrapers. Diamonds, opals, emeralds and sapphires studded their grand exteriors. The glittering beauty was breathtaking!

After surveying the beauty of my heavenly surroundings, I looked back and saw the face of sweet Jesus. Slowly and reverently I made my way toward Him. His beautiful, clear blue eyes glistened like a million crystal lights. It seemed all of heaven was ordained through His tender, eyes.

As I drew nigh to Jesus, I stretched my hands toward Him, and He stretched His loving arms toward me. As Jesus walked toward me, His pristine robe glistened with a heavenly radiance, like a million lights penetrating a dark tunnel. I couldn't take my eyes off Him.

As I continued to behold His majesty, I wanted to be with Jesus forever. I asked, "Lord, can I stay with you?" I knew this sinful world could never satisfy me again. Jesus replied: "I put a divine call on your life at the age of thirteen which you have not yet fulfilled."

As I tried to explain to the Lord why I hadn't obeyed the call on my life, He made no further comment. He needed no reminder.

I asked: "Could I lay my head on your bosom?" Smiling, the Lord replied, "When you return, my child, you may lay your head on my bosom." There was a brief silence -- my Lord seemed to look away beyond me. I tried to see where He was looking.

Something like a mirage appeared, slowly at first and then a mist-like scene appeared. I saw numerous structures.

In heaven, there's no such thing as time. It's just sort of like a dream, you just seem to think a thing and like a flash, it's there. I remembered what Jesus said to His disciples before He went back to heaven: "…in my Father's house are many mansions. I go to prepare a place for you…" (John 14:2).

And then, again in my humanness, I looked at the Lord like a child would look to his father and I said: "Lord, could I see my mansion?"

Blessed Jesus then dropped His arms to His side for a moment.

Then, He replied to me in His loving and longsuffering way:

> "You will see your mansion, but first let us talk about your call. You have been called of God. There are many people, who will need your ministry. As you stand and minister the gospel, you will not have to touch the sick; I will heal them in the midst of the congregation. Even as you stand to deliver the message that I give you, people will be healed. Miracles of healing and deliverance will come forth. As a result, people will give their hearts to God and will be brought into my kingdom."

He then paused. I was lost in what He was saying as He continued. "When your call has been answered and completed, then you will return to live with me forever."

Going to heaven after my work was completed made me think of my loved ones who had already gone on. And, I asked, "Lord, could I see my grandmother?"

My grandmother passed away at seventy-five. Her last words to me were, "I'll see you on the other side." I wondered about it. I assumed she was speaking of heaven.

When I saw my Grandmother, she was beautiful, youthful and radiant. Her peaceful face was that of a twenty-year-old woman. She was perfect in every way. The supernatural radiance about her could only have come from being in the presence of Jesus. We greeted each other with outstretched hands. It was a joyous reunion. The beauty of her vivid eyes and golden shoulder length hair startled me. She was wearing a lovely spotless white robe with a heavenly softness.

"I've been awaiting your arrival," she said in her familiar gentle manner. As we visited, it was evident that grandmother was well aware our family was not ready to meet Jesus, and she lovingly expressed her concern. Thankfully, those in heaven seemed to know what is happening on earth.

"Just" (grandmother's nickname for Justine, her daughter) is not ready to enter into heaven," she remarked wistfully. "Tell her if she will surrender her heart to God, she can come and live with Jesus and me forever. Tell the kids (my brothers and sisters) if they will give their hearts to God, they can come, and we can all live together forever."

What a "simple" profound message! How many times in Scripture did Jesus entreat us to believe upon Him as our Savior? Now from heaven, this message was repeated that none might enter except we ask Jesus into our hearts as our Savior.

Later, as a result of her pleading message, many of my family accepted Jesus as Lord and Savior.

During my short visit in heaven, grandmother and I conversed three times, and each time it was about our family.

I asked the Lord "Can I see my baby brother?"

John Thomas was the second born and died when he was only six weeks old. I had never seen him.

In the next instant, a young boy was standing at grandmother's side. In the natural he appeared to be twelve years old; I was completely surprised to see a twelve-year-old boy. I turned toward Jesus and said, "No, Lord, I want to see my baby brother."

Jesus said "This is your brother, John Thomas."

"I have been taking care of him," grandmother assured me.

Astonished that he had continued to grow while in heaven with his family, I looked again inquisitively at my brother. A beautiful smile spread across his little face. He had blonde hair and blue eyes, just like my other brothers. Joy filled me beyond measure.

I praise God for allowing me this privilege. I praise God there is going to be a reunion of all our loved ones one day soon. I will sing His praises in worship and adoration forever!

It was so wonderful to be standing in front of my grandmother and baby brother, knowing they were saved and were home with Jesus for all eternity. They had the same exquisite, heavenly glow about them, as did everyone in heaven.

There was a moment of silence as I stood looking at my little brother and my grandmother. Without saying a word, Jesus beckoned me toward him, and suddenly we were moving through glistening marble halls.

Soon we came to a magnificent, gem-studded mansion. It was like one big diamond, sparkling under thousands of lights. The very atmosphere surpassed all excitement or opulence that I've ever experienced on earth. This was my mansion!

"We did not go through any doors." ***HE <u>IS</u> THE DOOR!*** *(John 10:9).*

After the thrill of seeing my mansion, I expressed a desire to visit my grandmother's eternal home. This request was also granted. I found myself in an equally beautiful mansion with golden floors.

Everywhere we went, throughout all of Heaven, I could hear the melodious voices of the holy angels singing praises to the Eternal Father. Besides being enthralled with the beauty of it all, I was overcome with the love of God that filled heaven.

I remember walking on velvety-red roses, the size of watermelons. What amazed me was even after trampling the roses, they remained intact. Surely, this can happen only in heaven! Walking on heavenly green grass was more delightful than walking on plush carpet.

Although I had already received the Baptism of the Holy Spirit, that power could not compare to the tremendous power I experienced while standing before Jesus. Nothing in this life can compare with the love of Jesus. It was a profound experience of the fullness of goodness and mercy.

There's nothing more to be desired -- it's so beautiful!

In this life one cannot comprehend the majestic beauty of heaven. The Bible says, *"Eye hath not seen, nor ear heard, neither have entered into the heart of man, the things which God hath prepared for them that love him. But God hath revealed them unto us by his Spirit"* (1 Corinthians 2:9-10).

After the Lord had shown me heaven, He said, "This is already prepared for you, but you can't stay now."

His statement was like a thunder cloud that had fallen upon me. **"Jesus," I pleaded, "let me stay with you. I am so unhappy on earth...so miserable... I don't want to live!"**

He said to me, "**You cannot enter in until you have fulfilled your call, for only you can fulfill the call I have put upon your life."**

I was so disappointed, and yet, I knew it was a great privilege to be especially called by God.

We strolled along in a seemingly long silence. Then Jesus opened a hole in heaven to let me see my son, Rickey below, just two years old, sitting in his high chair, crying. Obviously, he needed his mother, and I knew I must go back for his sake.

Jesus encouraged me saying:

> **"Some people are called for various ministries; some are called to minister one-on-one, and others are called to minister to many: But, you are called to bring the multitudes to the Kingdom. You will not return until you have brought the multitudes.**
>
> **You were called for a creative miracle ministry to create body organs that are diseased or missing. You will never have to touch anyone. Always remember that I touched the people and sometimes I didn't.**
>
> **You will never see me, but I'll always be at your right side. You are never to fear man for what I have**

called you to do, and never doubt your calling. You have to return, but I've shown you heaven, and I've shown you enough that you will know that I am real."

Jesus is very real--alive and well! Thomas could not believe Jesus was real until he saw those prescious nail scarred hands. Yet, in heaven Jesus had no nail scars in His hands because all our afflictions and pain are healed once we reach heaven.

If we could all realize just how much Jesus really loves us and wants us to be happy with Him forever, we would never sin, and would prepare each day to meet Him for He said, "*You know not the day nor the hour when God will call us*."

Continuing, Jesus lovingly said to me, "**When you come back to live, you may stay forever. You may lay your head on my bosom. If every person on earth doubts your call, never forget what I have shown you."**

How I long for the day when I shall be with Jesus and my loved ones forever.

Jesus then added, **"On your return to earth, you will not see me, but I'll always be at your side.You are never to fear man for what I have called you to do, and never doubt your calling."**

I looked away for a moment, staring afar to absorb a last look at heaven. In the distance I saw angels teaching people to bow. I asked, "Jesus, why are those people so far away from you?"

He said to me, **"The angels are teaching them how to worship God."**

I silently wondered if they had been saved on their deathbeds. Strangely, it occurred to me that I didn't see the great crowds of people I had anticipated. Then I asked Him, "*Lord, where are all the people?"*

"The way was narrower than they thought," beloved Jesus replied in a saddened voice. **"Everything in heaven is perfect and pure, and no sin can enter here."**

I then asked our precious Lord, "Jesus, if I only have one message to stand and preach, what shall I preach?" He said:

"Tell my people to love me with all their heart, soul, mind and body, and to love each other as they love me. Great is my commandment that you love one another…" and He added, "More people will miss heaven because they do not have love one for another. I gave my blood and my life for people. Tell my people that they have never grasped the love I have for them."

Jesus took my right hand and said, **"Now I'm going to take you into another part of Heaven."** He had scarcely spoken and we were in the Throne Room of God, the Holy of Holies. The Throne Room was filled with bright white and bluish gray colors all at once. With His left hand, Jesus took my right hand as we stood in the majestic and holy room of God and said: **"Now, I am going to introduce you to my Father."**

I was in the Throne room; there I saw a large golden, stair-like arrangement and upon it sat God's Throne. Seated upon the Throne was the figure of a huge man with long white hair, like finely spun white wool. It was much longer than Jesus' hair.

His arms were laid across the golden arms of the Throne. His hands were as big as two of mine put together. There were no shoes on his feet, which appeared to be a man's size 13 or 14 in the natural. His robe was long and glistening white and lay in perfect folds across his large lap.

When I looked into his face, all I could see was a brilliant, blinding light as if I were looking at the blazing sun. It was just a ball of brightness.

I walked within six feet of the golden Throne.

Jesus looked at the Father with great love, reverencing His very name as the Father of the entire universe. God's son, Jesus, stood in total submission and reverence to the Father. Jesus turned again to look at the Creator, our heavenly Father, sitting on the magnificent throne.

When God leaned forward, He stretched both of His arms toward me. His robe glistened. Jesus' voice was always soft and gentle while He was giving me the tour of heaven. But when God spoke (to me), it sounded like a million jets taking off, all at the same time. All of heaven was shaken and felt the thunder with the sound of His voice, and yet it was full of love.

This is what God said to me: **"I have made provision for everything that you will ever need on earth, and all you will ever have to do is to reach out and take it."**

This fulfills scripture in the Old Testament which states, "*...All the silver is mine and all the gold is mine, and I own the cattle on a thousand hills*" (Psalms 50:10).

God said nothing more to me, and Jesus and I departed. Just after leaving the Throne Room, Jesus made a promise to me saying that if I would believe Him, whatever I spoke with my lips, He would perform.

It was time for my departure. As I started to leave, desiring another glimpse of Jesus, I looked into His beautiful, liquid blue eyes. Then, turning around, I saw my grandmother nod her head and smile as she said, "I will await your arrival."

Next I looked at my baby brother, John Thomas, and he smiled as if to say, "I, too, will be awaiting your return."

I started to leave, but not without a twinge of sadness, although I had been given the assurance I would definitely be returning one day to stay forever and ever. A gate swung open as thousands of angels sang, ushering me on my way. I began descending through the sky, drifting through the fluffy white clouds.

The next thing I knew I was coming down through the ceiling at the doctor's office. As I began to regain consciousness, I noticed a woman leaning over me crying, a woman whom I had led to the Lord some time before.

In my "out-of-body state," I tried to tell her I was indeed on my way back. I wanted to cry out, "Don't cry. I'm on my way back," but she couldn't hear me. Next, I felt my spirit re-enter my body. I was very conscious that I was once again on the doctor's table.

The last thing the Lord said to me was, **"When you return to earth, there will not be any scars on your heart. It will be like the heart of a thirteen-year-old girl."**

Meanwhile, during my visit to heaven, the doctor called for an ambulance. I was soon on my way to the hospital. The ambulance screamed down the busy streets of Dallas carrying me to Steven's Park Hospital accompanied by my doctor.

Other doctors said among themselves that it was impossible for me to have had a heart attack. My doctor insisted that I had indeed collapsed with a cardiac arrest. The hospital doctors could not be convinced, even in light of the tests. "This woman could not possibly have sustained two heart attacks, not even one, because her heart is beating as soundly as a thirteen year old child's," said one of the emergency room physicians, echoing God's very words to me in heaven.

Lying in my bed, I could hear the doctors arguing. I asked the nurse to tell my doctor I wanted to tell him something very important. When the doctor came to my bedside, I told him about my celestial visit, and how Jesus had healed my heart. He told me it would be like that of a thirteen year-old child. The doctor listened with obvious astonishment. He responded by saying, "That is wonderful, but you better remain in the hospital for a few more days."

At the prescribed time, they released me. I continued my life as a wife and mother as usual, raising my young son, and knowing in my heart that my life was soon to turn around.

Doctor's Office where Loretta encountered her Heavenly experience. (Now a dental clinic.)

3

THE EARLY YEARS

Rosston, Arkansas was a quiet rural area, about a third of the way between Texarkana and Pine Bluff. It is on the map, but not in bold letters. Ordinarily it was so quiet all you ever heard was the crowing of roosters and the mooing of cows. However, if you visited the farm of Justine and Cleve Chamberlain, the noise of their youngsters could drown out a whole herd of cattle!

My twin sister, Bernice and I were born in Rosston. I was born three minutes after Bernice, number 9, becoming the tenth of the Chamberlain children. With two sets of twins—two boys and two girls—we quickly became a big family, eventually numbering seventeen. If little John Thomas, who was the second born had not died as a baby at six weeks old, we would have totaled fifteen children.

Although we did not have money for toys and bicycles like our friends, we were healthy and had lots of fun together. Living on a small farm, there were always chores. Nevertheless, despite all the work, we found time to ride horses and play games. With eight boys and six girls, we always had enough for our own softball and racing teams.

In football season, my brothers would "recruit" their sisters to make their football team complete. Many evenings after supper, Mother would come out to the porch and watch us as we formed teams to play games in our huge front yard.

Life was not easy for us, especially for my precious mother. The burden fell solely on her shoulders. She was a hard worker; my alcoholic father worked in construction and traveled around the state to find work. Sadly, he contributed little to the rearing of his children.

Life without a devoted father made it extremely hard for our mother. Yet, as children, we found our happiness in the closeness of a large family and a mother who poured her love and care upon us in spite of deprivation and hard work.

Even though we did not have the household appliances that most families had, mother insisted we wear clean clothing everyday. I'm sure you remember how mothers were about "clean underwear" back in those days. Not only did we not have a washing machine or dryer, mother was meticulous about our clothes being clean.

Many times, my sisters and I played around mother's feet while she starched and ironed our mountain of clothes. She always said, "Even though we are poor, we can still be clean." My sisters and I were taught at an early age to help with washing and ironing. Although these were not chores that I particularly enjoyed, everyone had to help with the housework. It was just a way of life for all of us.

Each day, in our freshly starched clothes and with our homemade lunch buckets, we left the farm to catch the school bus into Prescott.

It was about an hour's drive. I can still see in my mind's eye how mother would stand in her flour sack dress and fresh apron, and faithfully wave us good-bye. When we returned from school, she was at the bus stop waiting to ensure our safety home. It was about a quarter mile from the bus to the house.

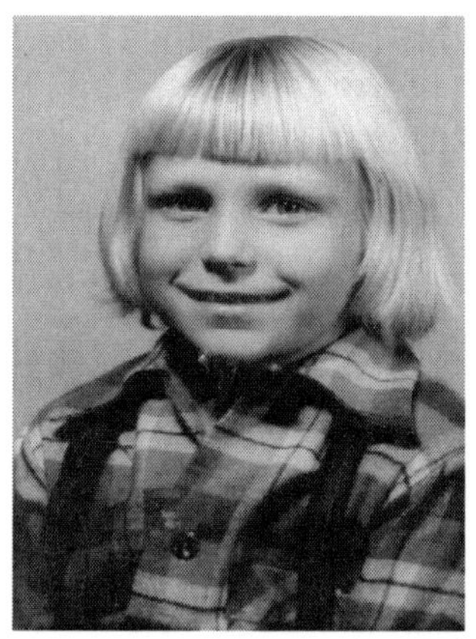
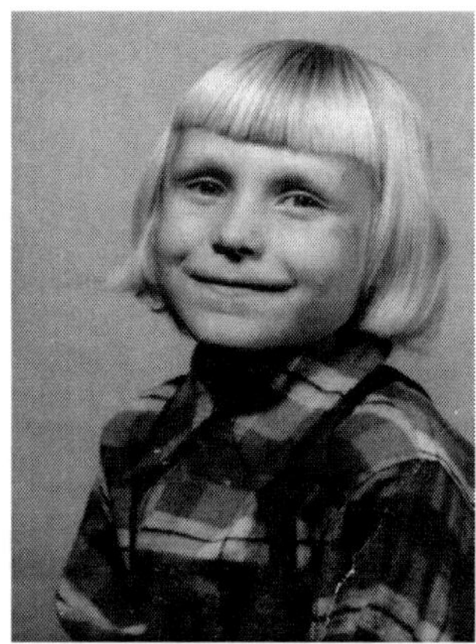

Loretta (left) and Bernice.

My twin sister Bernice and I enjoyed a special kind of fun and tricks on the bus ride and in school that only twins share.

We were identical twins and neither our father nor our relatives could tell us apart. As youngsters daddy called us both "Baby" since he was never sure to whom he was speaking. But as we grew older, there began to be a great deal of difference in our physical appearance.

Bernice was always up to something. I make no confession of guilt but I really enjoyed her antics and we had a lot of harmless fun. What one didn't think of, the other one did.

I recall with a smile one time when daddy gave Bernice a dollar. And knowing daddy could not tell us apart, Bernice would snuggle up to him a little bit later and go ask innocently for another dollar. He would give it to her, thinking he was giving it to me. She was the one who always asked because she seemed to be more successful than I.

The down side of our shenanigans was, he always spanked me, thinking I was Bernice, and she never tried to clarify the mistake. There were definitely times that our dual identity was a lot harder on me than her.

Nevertheless, we loved each other dearly; the good and the bad always seemed to balance out. I remember well an incident in the first grade. The teacher was going to spank me because I would not answer her when she called on me. She thought I was stubborn, but actually, I was too bashful to speak up.

On this day, she thought she would teach me a lesson for my "stubbornness" and was in the process of taking a switch to me. (This was before the "child abuse" thing became an item). My sister, looking on in sheer horror, ran up and yanked the switch out of the teacher's hand, broke it, threw it on the floor and jumped in front of me. With tears in her eyes, she said defiantly, "You're gonna have to go through me first!"

The teacher was obviously so shocked by Bernice's boldness that she changed her mind and decided that I didn't need a spanking. This is just one example of many when we felt we had to stick together.

We still laugh about the different antics we got into while riding the school bus to the Prescott Arkansas School. It took an hour to get there, and that was too much time for Bernice to go without mischief. She would sit still as long as possible, then she would decide to stir up a little excitement. She was an expert at throwing spitballs.

Expert as she was though, she never got away with it. The bus driver would make her come down to the front of the bus and sit by him. And you guessed it. I would take the front seat instead and the driver never knew the difference.

He'd say to me, thinking I was Bernice, "You should be more like your sister." I'd sit in the front seat and giggle and Bernice would be doubled up in the back laughing her head off. Between my twin's spitballs and water gun, I always had a front seat and a clear view of the road ahead. On the other hand, the bus driver gave one of my other sisters, Marilyn, a silver dollar for good behavior.

Since there were fourteen Chamberlain children, there were always several of us on the school bus. My brother Bo used a different kind of tactic to bug the bus driver. Many times, when we stopped in the smaller villages for more passengers, he would slip out the back door of the bus and sneak away to spend the day in town. Being undetected, he would catch the school bus when it came by in the afternoon and mother would never know he had skipped school that day.

Sometimes he would get off at a closer stop and go back home and say he was sick. And very dutifully, mom would give him the family remedy for all ills— castor oil. Later, Bo would confess to us that the day out of school was worth any punishment. Being "loyal sisters," we never told on him. There were other times when we needed his loyalty. Since we were nine and ten in the birthing order, Bernice and I probably gave the most trouble.

I remember another time when a boy at school pulled my hair. Now, remember, I was the "shy" one. As I stood up, Bernice picked him up like he was a feather and threw him outdoors into a pile of gravel. No one, including the guilty boy would dare tell the teachers who did it. They were all afraid of Bernice. Later, he turned out to be our best friend in school.

We looked forward to getting home after school, always knowing we would have a hot meal waiting for us. Mother alone made our drafty little farmhouse cozy with a good hot meal and the flame of her devotion. We knew that her children meant everything to her, and we loved her dearly.

We all pitched in together farming the land and growing most of our own food. The summers were spent canning fruits and vegetables. I especially remember the cold winter days after school when our long kitchen table would be piled high with the food that we had helped mother preserve the previous summer. There was always plenty for everyone; we never lacked for food or warmth.

We were not necessarily an affectionate family, but no one could have had a more considerate, devoted mother than we had. We knew we meant everything to her, and we all, somehow, knew that we were very lucky to have her for our mother.

WE ALL PITCHED IN AND WORKED THE FARM

We worked hard on the farm. Each of the boys was assigned his tasks to keep the farm running smoothly. The girls helped mother with the washing, ironing, cleaning and all the household chores.

We had a few cows and their calves. They made lots of good milk and butter.

Sometimes we would try to ride the calves, pretending they were horses. At other times we would ride the mule that was normally used for plowing the fields. This usually worked out better than the little calves.

With our own cows and chickens, and an occasional deer that the boys would bring in from hunting, we had lots of good food. Mother milked the cows and made butter in a big ole' crock. In spite of the hard work, these were special times that, in years to come, would warmly remind us of our love for one another, and occasionally make us laugh.

The best thing about living in Arkansas was our family. I loved my brothers and sisters; we enjoyed life together. But in my heart, I knew something was missing in my life. I felt an emptiness and yearned for something that I could not explain to anyone, nor did I try since I did not understand these feelings myself. Little did I know then what God had in store for me, and how my life would soon change.

THE NEW TV

One day we were outside playing and my mother came running to tell us that daddy had bought a TV and was on his way home with it. We couldn't wait for him to come—we were all so excited to see this wonderful new box. It seemed like a longer wait than it really was, but eventually my daddy arrived with this mysterious new TV.

After daddy got it all hooked up, I'll never forget the first thing we saw on our new TV. It was a man under a huge tent preaching and praying for people in wheelchairs and crutches and others with all kinds of afflictions. Young as I was, I could see their faces full of pain, and seemingly hopelessness.

But then this "healing evangelist," whom I later learned was Reverend Oral Roberts, would pray for them and they would come out of their chairs.

I saw parents bring their small children, and after Reverend Roberts prayed for them, I saw them run down that ramp that was at the front of the tent. This made a tremendous impression on me. I remember how the tears ran down my face as I watched.

My mother, being very concerned, asked me what was wrong. I said, "Someday, this is what I want to do with my life." She seemed overly concerned and stayed close to me.

I watched every time I knew Reverend Roberts would be on the TV. I loved to hear him preach and see him pray for people. I remember the joy on the faces of those people as they were healed from their pain. Even when people didn't seem to be healed immediately, I knew in my heart that God could heal and perform miracles as I had witnessed on TV that day.

Like Mary, Mother of Jesus, I kept all this in my heart and knew that one day I would pray for people, and they would be healed.

We continued to live on the farm in Arkansas until I was in my early-teens. We still saw little of my father who continued to travel and work in construction in various cities. He had been in Dallas for a number of months, only coming home periodically to be with the family.

It was on one of his trips home that he and mother decided that the family would move to Dallas. They felt that life would not be so hard in the big city as it had been on the farm, especially for our mother. Plus, it would be wonderful to live closer to our brothers and sisters and their families.

So it was an adventure for the "clan" to move to Big "D". The things that I would soon experience in Dallas would be so overwhelming that, even now, as I look back, I have to believe that only God could have allowed such life-changing circumstances.

But then, my encounter with God when I was only five years old, was an experience that has guided me through every dilemma that I faced, large or small. Truly, there is somebody up there!

My family never attended church, but Otis, one of my older brothers, and his family did. After our family moved to Dallas, they kept inviting me to go to church with them. All I really knew about it was that it was one of those "Liberal" churches.

As a teen-ager and very full of my own ideas, I just wasn't the slightest bit interested. I turned a deaf ear to their invitations and nonchalantly carried on with my new life in Dallas, but God paid no attention to my "deaf ear." Instead, He gave Otis a "burden" for me. Otis was not one to be put off so easily. He began to double his efforts to get me to church and "get me saved."

I couldn't understand why Otis was so determined to "get me saved," as he put it. Then one day I learned from one of my siblings that Otis had said: "The Lord has told me that Loretta will, one day, be a minister." And further he said, "God has told me to go on a fast and pray and intercede until God saves her and baptizes her with this "Holy Spirit" thing. I did not know about the things he was talking about.

But I did know that Otis was a very dedicated Christian. I knew he was a man of prayer, but when he added that "fasting" and "Holy Spirit" stuff, things began to happen. I soon learned what power there is in fasting and all the other stuff he had added.

Not knowing it was the forty-second day of Otis' fast, I consented to go to church with Otis and his family that night. It was nothing new for Otis and his family, but I didn't have the slightest idea what to expect. I was only thirteen years of age. I enjoyed the music, the people were friendly and there was an air of expectancy and excitement.

The minister's sermon was on "How Much Jesus Loves You." Since my own father had never told me he loved me, the message spoke to my heart. I wanted to know more about a Jesus that could love me in the way the minister was speaking about.

Suddenly, I got up out of the pew and ran down to the altar right in the middle of the minister's sermon. I fell on my knees with tears running down my face and I cried out: "I want Jesus!"

Soon Otis and the whole church were right behind me rejoicing and praising the Lord. At that moment, it was as though a great weight had been lifted from my entire being, and I felt a peace, and a love, and a calmness I had never known. The emptiness and loneliness I had felt all my life was gone and I was filled with a kind of liquid joy. I knew this was what I had been searching for all my life! I was happier than I had ever been!

I was "born again." God became more than my heavenly father. He became my guiding hand like an earthly father is supposed to be.

Otis and the entire church rejoiced with me and received me into the church with more love and joy than I had ever known.

As the Bible says, I became "a new creation in Christ Jesus." To say the least, my whole life changed in moments – but it was only the beginning. This new experience happened in an instant, but I began to learn it would take the rest of my life to learn and live it out.

Otis, his family and the entire church became my church and family. I became what some people refer to as a "fanatic"!

God graciously added to my life friends who treated me like a "new born baby" and actually that is what I was spiritually. Actually, with all the other various kinds of feelings I was a little fearful.

Then very shortly after this most glorious night of transformation of my life, the Holy Spirit became my Teacher.

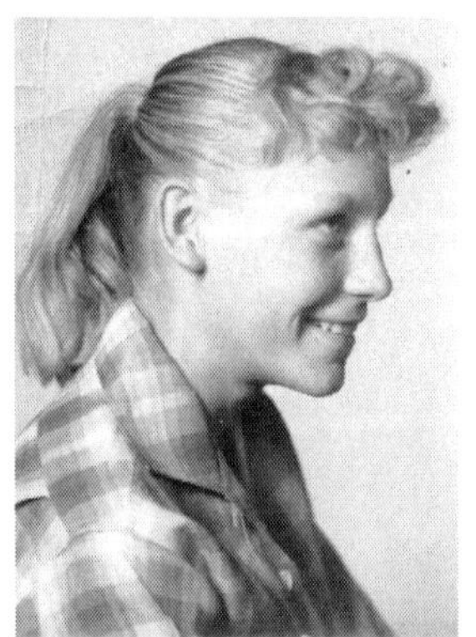

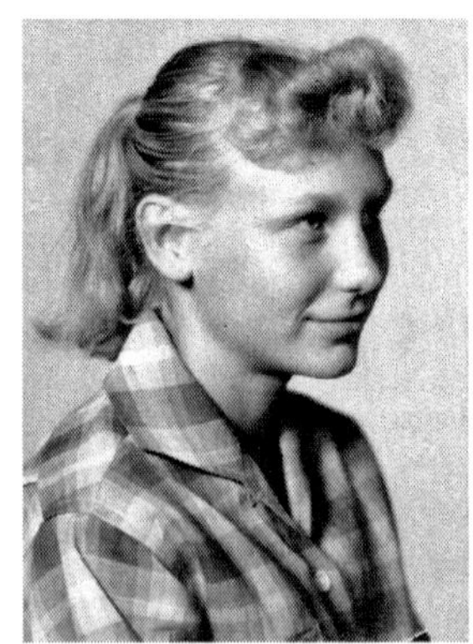

Loretta (left) and Bernice as teenagers.

4

THE "TEACHER"

I continued to go to church with Otis and his family. I began to read and learn the Bible. I was being schooled in truths that would, in the future, carry me through all the things in life that I didn't foresee or expect to happen. Now that I had given my heart to Jesus, the scales were being removed from my eyes. I knew without a shadow of a doubt, that there was an Almighty God in the heavens.

Two nights later, I had an incredibly unique and wonderful experience. I was lying in my bed, about to drift off to sleep when a figure walked into my bedroom and held out to me a white Bible. At first, I was startled, but suddenly a gentle calm came over me, and I stretched out my hand to receive the Bible.

And as I did, Jesus said, "I am calling you to do a work for me that will stretch around the world. I am commissioning you to preach my Gospel and heal the people as I did when I was on earth."

He then showed me a vision of thousands of people and said, "Soon, these whom you see will be the people to whom you will minister."

I sat up in bed and brushed my eyes and reached out again to take the white Bible as He continued: "And as you stand and preach the word of God, I will heal people as they sit in the congregation."

Remember now, I was a brand new Christian and I didn't know what, or how, to preach, or what to say. To say the least, such a statement overwhelmed me. I was scared and did not understand nor comprehend this vision. I thought surely I must be dreaming, but I knew deep down in my spirit that this was very real and powerful. And still, I said: "Lord, I don't know how to preach." And He whispered very softly, "The Holy Spirit will teach you."

I found myself hearing those words over and over in my spirit, "The Holy Spirit will teach you." And I thought, *"Who is the Holy Spirit and how can He teach me?"*

I opened my Bible and read: *"...wait for the promise of the Father which saith he, ye have heard of me, for John truly baptized with water; but ye shall be baptized with the Holy Spirit not many days hence"* (Acts 1-5).

I raised my hands and began to quietly praise the Lord. And as I continued to praise and worship the Lord, He again reminded me of my call to preach and to do all He said that I would do because "He would teach me." And then every time I would open my mouth to praise Him, nothing but a heavenly language would come out. This lasted throughout the night and the next day.

It was a glorious experience and I have felt the influence of the Holy Spirit's presence in my life ever since.

Truly, He has become THE TEACHER in my life and ministry. He is doing what He promised to do.

I have found that the Holy Spirit is the One called along side to help me in all that I do.

In Romans 8:26-28 He says:

> *Likewise the Spirit also helpeth our infirmities: for we know not what we could pray for as we ought: but the Spirit Himself maketh intercession for us with groanings which cannot be uttered. And he that searcheth the hearts knoweth what is the mind of the*

Spirit, because he maketh intercession for the saints according to the will of God.

I was very conscious of the fact that I did not receive a good education early on, having attended a one-room school in Arkansas. Because of my lack of education, and sometimes the hardness of my own heart, it would take many years of hard knocks and much learning for me to finally and totally surrender all to my Gracious God.

However through the years, He has done exactly what He said He would do. He has been and will continue to be my Teacher.

I had no encouragement in my home as far as my Christian walk was concerned. I would attempt to talk to my parents about my call, but they couldn't cope with this. It was foreign to them. My family called my church a "holy-roller" church.

My daddy said, "Loretta, this is the worst thing you could have gotten into," and he threatened to "beat me to death" if I went back to that church. He knew that my brother Otis had been saved and was filled with the Holy Spirit, but that was of little concern to him, since Otis was married and lived away from home.

The church I attended was a revival center and conducted services every night. Knowing full well my father's threats, I continued to go to church every night. Even though my mother didn't understand, she protected me from my dad, and he never carried out his threats.

I could walk to church since it was about ten blocks from our house. Sometimes the services would last until eleven o'clock. And when the service was over, I would run home and get in bed so my dad would not know that I had been out.

Some of the church members would offer to take me home, but I didn't want the unnecessary noise of car doors and engines to wake my dad.

Is Anybody Up There?

This was many years ago, when it was still safe to walk day or night. Yet, sometimes it was scary, but I knew how to pray for the angels to surround me and take charge over me. The Lord assured me they were there, even though I couldn't see them. I learned very early that I could pray and run at the same time. And as I ran, I learned also how to talk to God as though we two were the only two out at night.

In those early, sometimes very hard years, I really learned how valuable it was to know God in the dimension of the Holy Spirit. The Baptism in the Holy Spirit was the one experience that made me know beyond a shadow of a doubt that all of my other experiences in God were real and valid.

This experience is spoken of in the New Testament in the Second Chapter of the Acts of the Apostles. The outpouring of the Holy Spirit was promised by Jesus in St. John's Gospel, chapters 14, 15, 16, and Luke 24:48.

Jesus Himself said:

> *But the Comforter, which is the Holy Ghost, Whom the Father will send in my name, shall teach you all things, and bring all things to your remembrance, whatsoever I said unto you (John 14:26).*

In those early and growing years, I leaned how valuable it was to know God in the dimension of the Holy Spirit. The Baptism in the Holy Spirit is the one experience that makes me know beyond a shadow of a doubt that all of my other experiences in God were real and valid, and continue to be.

This is what He promised and this is what He has done for me all through the years.

The Psalmist said: "*He magnifies His Word above His name*" (Psalm 138:2).

5

THE JANITOR AND THE DRUMMER

To me, as a thirteen-year-old girl, God's call on my life did not seem like an impossible task. In my childlike mind, trusting was not a question of doubt. It was as simple as "yes, Lord." As an adult, I might not have surrendered so willingly.

Childlike faith seems to disappear when we cut our "wisdom teeth." God was about to entrust me with a ministry. If I were to succeed, I would have to trust and obey God, and dedicate my very heart and soul to Him. He would have to be my total Source and my Strength.

King David, called and anointed of God in his youth, began by continuing to minister to the sheep. Slaying giants came a bit later. But God had armed him, and given him an anointing and strength. And, it was only in God's strength, and only by the anointing of God's Holy Spirit, that He armed me.

My heart was filled with love for Jesus, and I wanted to serve Him.

I began by volunteering my help at church. I felt that if I could spend more time in the house of God, that somehow I would be closer to God and that He would reappear and tell me what I was to do. However, that did not exactly happen as I expected.

One time, the church I attended needed a janitor and I "volunteered" for the job, and got it. I was probably the only volunteer. My zeal no doubt surprised the pastor, for he cheerfully agreed to let me clean the church. I'm sure he saw it as an emptying of myself in sweet devotion and by doing so, the perfecting came.

It took me a while to learn how one advances in the kingdom — it's as Jesus said: *...but whosoever will be great among you, let him be your minister. And whosoever will be chief among you, let him be your servant: Even as the Son of man came not to be ministered unto, but to minister, and to give his life as a ransom for many (Matthew 20:26-28).*

Some time later, I learned that the drummer in the church orchestra was going to leave Dallas to move back to Arkansas. He informed the Pastor of his intended move, and at Sunday service the Pastor asked the congregation, "Does anyone play the drums?"

Remembering a previous sermon when the Pastor had stressed that God can do anything, I stood up and boldly said, "I can," and made my way to the altar under the dubious eyes of the congregation. I'm sure some silently questioned the talent of this pretty, young teenager. Even the Pastor registered surprise, no doubt thinking to himself, "*I should have known Loretta would speak up*."

With raised eyebrows, he turned to me and said, "I didn't know you could play the drums, Loretta." "Well," I said with some sort of confidence, "I don't know how to play the drums, but if you will anoint my hands with oil and pray, then I will be able to play the drums."

Without questioning my holy boldness, he complied with my request. I sat down and began playing—very well I might add.

God performed a wonderful miracle. He provided me with a set of drums, and I became a talented drummer and played in the orchestra for three years.

It wasn't long before I began praying for people at the altar. I didn't realize God had already begun using me in a healing ministry until different ones came to me later, and told me how God had healed them after I prayed for them.

My new found church life was the greatest thing that had ever happened to me. I studied hard, and later I taught Sunday school, and also worked in the office. Jesus was gently nudging me forward on the training field, the church where I was born again. One can have no better training than by the Lord Himself.

The disciples learned by sitting at the feet of Jesus. And now He was establishing His Word in my heart and with the people. I grew with joyous excitement seeing the Lord at work as He had promised when He appeared to me that glorious night in my room.

One of the functions of the Holy Spirit in our lives is to teach us. And He was teaching me day by day—sometimes the lessons were very hard, but I always found His Grace sufficient.

The Chamberlain Family

Back Row Left to Right: Hollis, Jerry, Freeman (Bo), Otis, Ron, Charlie

Middle Row Left to Right: Wallace, Marilyn, Charlotte, Kenneth

Seated on First Row, Left to Right: Loretta, Father (Cleve), Mother (Justine), June.

Standing: Doris (left) Bernice (right)

6

"BIG D" – ALMOST TOO BIG

Even though Jesus had changed my life, I had so much to learn in the big city. High School in Dallas was a traumatic experience for me and my twin sister. We had been brought up in a much smaller school in Arkansas, and had always been in the same classes. We also enjoyed a certain amount of popularity back home, but here, in this BIG Dallas high school, we felt like country bumpkins.

Very soon, I became more and more introverted. I literally stood behind Bernice and depended upon her to make all my decisions for me. Because of this, the school officials felt that Bernice and I should not be in the same classes, so they separated us. To us it felt like the Siamese twins must have felt when separated. I was shy and very lonely. As a result I could not make many friends.

This big change had its influence on my grades. I was always scared that the teachers would call on me; and rather than stand in front of the class to recite, I would say, "I don't know".

The one bright spot in my life at this place in my life was my newfound salvation. All I wanted to do was read my Bible and go to church—it seemed like such a haven from "the country bumpkin" image.

However, I made the mistake that many new converts make—instead of being a good example of "a new creation" in Christ, my grades went down the drain.

Instead of paying attention to the teachers, I would often read my Bible in the classroom. As a result, I failed my English courses due to my own inattention. However, my mother took charge when my teachers sent home a failing slip. She personally saw to it that I attended summer school to take courses that I had failed. I only wish I'd had more wisdom at the time.

Eventually, much to my parent's disapproval, I quit school altogether to follow my dreams. But I quickly learned that a person can be ever so "born again," but without the discipline to come under the authority of those over you, you are doomed for failure.

Very soon, I realized I had to face up to my disobedience, my weaknesses and particularly my shyness and give everything to the Lord and allow Him to redeem it. And redeem it He did. I later passed an equivalency test and enrolled in college, taking courses at night to continue my education.

I look back to those awkward years and I marvel at God's redeeming Grace and how He transformed me from a shy, insecure, lonely teen-ager into a minister who loves crowds of people, large or small. Sharing my testimony and ministering healing miracles to the lost and hurting, is my passion.

Loretta's parents Cleve and Justine Chamberlain on their 50th Wedding Anniversary.

7

MY FLASH VISION OF HELL

At seventeen, I continued to "toy" with serving the Lord my way. I was then assisting an evangelist in Dallas. After a while, I began to experience a very uncomfortable feeling when I was in the company of her organist. It soon became obvious that she did not like me. It was a situation over which I had no control. And I began to have an attitude toward her that I knew was not of God. I didn't know how to change it, but God knew.

He taught me in an extremely graphic way how important His commandments are to our salvation, His commandment to:

...Love your enemies, bless them that curse you, do good to them that hate you, and pray for them which despitefully use you, and persecute you...(Matthew 5:44).

One Sunday, after returning home from church, I walked into my bedroom and sat on the bed to take off my shoes when suddenly I was overtaken with a flash vision of hell! It was totally unexpected, very short and very real.

I felt icy cold as the vision became more vivid. I felt as though I was being pulled inside something like a television screen. I saw great fiery flames enveloping lost souls who struggled in futility to escape the torturous flames.

Their wretched, burned faces were covered with slithering worms; I saw their agony and heard their piercing screams as they bit their tongues, and the blood streamed out of their mouths.

There were young people with yellow, purple, and blue hair in weird styles, groping blindly at one another. Many heads were shaven and colored in eerie designs. And then the vision flashed away.

Later, much to my amazement, I saw these same kinds of weird, colored hair styles being worn by those who rebelled against home, government and all that is decent and moral. Believe me, the idea is from the pits of hell.

The vision disappeared in a flash, as it had appeared. I was still sitting on the side of my bed with my shoes off and the palms of my hands so wet that perspiration had dripped off my fingers into little pools all around me.

I was terrified. I asked, "Why? What was it about?" Then Jesus appeared at my side and said, **"Loretta, this is where you will go if you have hate in your heart."** *"Hate?"* I asked in wonderment. And He opened my eyes to the scripture in Mark where He said:

> It is better for you to enter the kingdom of God with one eye than to have two eyes and be thrown into hell, where their worm does not die, and the fire is not quenched (Mark 9:47-48).

Suddenly, He called the evangelist's organist by name.

I sat there dazed — I didn't realize I actually hated her. I just thought I was hurt because of some unfortunate experiences, and I felt justified in disliking her.

This was a chilling lesson, and I did some heavy repenting. Hell is not a place I want to go.

This was a vivid, graphic lesson from Jesus that we must not hate or harbor a grudge against anyone. Only God is the Judge, and we must forgive and strive daily to live our lives with a pure heart.

I will never forget such a powerful vision and I will include in my preaching ministry that hell is real and "*...except ye repent, ye shall all likewise perish*" (Luke 13:3).

8

WEDDING BELLS

It was only one day before my wedding, when I began to experience feelings of fear and uncertainty. At the time, I was working for a couple in their ministry, and I confided my feelings to them. Actually, I told them I had changed my mind and did not want to get married. But they assured me that these feelings were normal and that everything would work out for "this was God's will."

The wedding was to be informal with only my minister friends who were to perform the ceremony. My financé and I were at the church at the scheduled time. But no one else was there.

It was getting late, when my friends finally showed up with the sad news that they were not licensed in Texas and could not perform the ceremony. That should have confirmed my feelings of canceling the wedding, but my fiancé was insistent.

After racking my brain, I remembered my good friends, Walt and Betty Mills, and I thought, *If they will perform the ceremony, then it must be God's will.*

Only God knows how much trouble and heartache I could have saved myself if I had listened to my own spirit and not taken the advice of well-meaning friends. But we all are blessed with 20/20 hindsight, I guess.

We arrived after midnight at the Mills' home. We continued knocking on the door until they finally answered. Walt, sleepy-eyed, appeared in his robe. Obviously, we had awakened them. We asked Walt if he could marry us. He very graciously asked us in and went to awaken Betty.

Walt performed the ceremony and Betty acted as the witness. After all the congratulations, good wishes and their prayers, we left to spend our "honeymoon night" at the local Holiday Inn.

I learned the next day that we would not be going on a honeymoon trip since my new husband had lost his job the previous week, (a small fact he failed to share with me). So, our honeymoon cottage was a rented apartment, and even that was by faith.

It is amazing the resilience young people have. My new husband called his boss on his old job the following Monday and was hired back—a direct answer to our prayers. So, rocky as it was, we were now on the road to a new life together.

I was a young bride of nineteen, and happily looked forward to starting a family. We were serving the Lord "afar off," for I had really put God's call on the back burner. Right now I wanted to have a marriage and children. To me, having children was a marvelous fulfillment of marriage. However, time marched on and no children were forthcoming.

After some time, I went to the doctor for a checkup and was told that I would not be able to have any children. I was terribly distressed.

To me, a marriage without children would be incomplete. I would have accepted this disappointment had I not remembered the Lord's words: *"Hitherto have ye asked nothing in my name: ask, and ye shall receive, that your joy may be full" (John 16:24).*

So with complete confidence in His Word, I prayed these words back to God and asked the Lord to give us a son.

My answer came two years later in the form of a beautiful little boy. Our son, Rickey Lee, was born on December 31, 1966.

It was eighteen degrees below zero that day when I called my mother to tell her the good news. But, she already knew, because my identical twin sister, Bernice (who was several hundred miles away from me), had called my mother earlier to tell her that she began to experience labor pains and had to leave work. Because we always seemed to do things together, this meant that Loretta would soon be calling with word of her delivery.

When the nurse brought Rickey to me the first time, he was like a bundle of sunshine, so small and so sweet. Each day, I held him as God's gift to me. And I thanked God each day for this precious gift of life, not realizing how I would soon have to trust the Lord for his very life.

My mother came and stayed with me two weeks which was a lifesaver.

HEARTACHES AND TRIALS....

"In the world, ye shall have tribulation; but be of good cheer; I have overcome the world"(John 16:33).

My marriage was not a happy one, and began to deteriorate with the daily pressures of married life. My husband could not seem to cope with a wife and child, and everyday rigors of life. Trying to continue our lives together seemed impossible. So, in 1969, I filed for divorce and was granted custody of our son, Rickey.

This was not unexpected. As I have mentioned before, I felt in my spirit the day before the wedding (three years before) that I should cancel the wedding. Many assured me it was only normal to feel this way. They said that I had all the feelings of doubt, frustration, and fear – all of which are normal for a young bride to feel. So we proceeded with the wedding, knowing in my spirit I should not.

It was a rocky three years and I choose not to rehash it. It was a mistake. Now, I have to make the best of it, and try to make a life for Rickey and I.

Being divorced made it extra hard. I had the full burden of caring for Rickey, both physically and financially.

Rickey at two years old.

9

A BLOCKBUSTER AND SPECIAL SCHOOLS

In early 1974, when Rickey was only seven, I began to notice that he had learning problems. It was hard to admit that there was a problem, but I knew there was really no other option. So I entered him into the Scottish Rite Hospital in Dallas, Texas. It is recognized as one of the best facilities for what Rickey needed.

I'll never forget the day the doctors at the Scottish Rite Hospital told me the results of Rickey's examination. It was a day like many other days in Dallas, sunny, birds singing in the trees, and all seemed well. I was sitting in the outer office right by the door, waiting anxiously for the results of the testing and evaluation session.

To this point, I thought I was the happiest mother alive. Then, suddenly, the door opened and all I really remember the doctor saying was..."I'm sorry, Ms. Blasingame, your son has tested educationally retarded."

His words were like a blockbuster in my mind. Everything went black. I was out for a few minutes. When I came to, the doctor was handing me a glass of water. I looked at him blankly, and he asked in amazement, "Ms. Blasingame, didn't you already know this?" I just stared at him. Haltingly, he went on, "Your uh, son should be, uh... placed in Terrell...."

"In Terrell?", I thought, "*Terrell is a hospital outside of Dallas for mentally challenged children!*"

The doctor's next words jolted me back into reality, and I heard the doctor saying, "Rickey's brain is not developing; in fact, by the time he is eighteen, he will not know who he is or who you are!"

My heart had never known such pain. Rickey was the joy of my life. Somehow I got to my car. As I stood there feeling alone and forsaken, I looked up at the sky; it was a beautiful blue, and the clouds looked like giant pieces of popcorn floating aimlessly about.

As I searched the heavens, it was like I was a child again in the fields of my family home in Arkansas when I cried out, "***Is anybody up there?" And the answer came, "I am here. I am God!"***

I needed the reassurance of my early childhood experience right now. And God answered me. It wasn't audible like before, but I had been walking with God for a number of years, and I was learning to hear Him speak to my spirit. And now, I heard Him gently saying, "Trust Me."

I think I felt like Jesus must have felt when He turned to His disciples and asked, "*Will you also go away*?"

At this point there was no one in the world I could go to for an answer. So, standing there in that hospital parking lot, I lifted my eyes heavenward again. I promised God I would dedicate my life to rearing my son into becoming a healthy and normal child. I said, "God, I do trust you, and I believe you for a miracle. All I ask is that you will give me the strength, grace, faith, and patience."

Instead of placing Rickey in a school for the retarded as the doctor suggested, I enrolled him in the Dallas Academy School in Dallas, Texas. My brothers and sisters, most of us, finished our elementary and high schooling in Dallas. So, I knew Dallas had excellent schools.

A Blockbuster and Special Schools

Again, Rickey was evaluated at the new school and placed in classes for the educationally retarded. Records showed that, when compared to educationally retarded students, Rickey scored below seventy percent in independent functioning; physical development; language development; numbers and time; vocation activity; self-direction; and socialization.

The years 1973 through 1977 were all the same – trying to work, running to school, sometimes several times a day; at times, battling loneliness and praying…a lot. I continually sought God for a miracle.

There were times when I worked two jobs to pay for the special food, schooling and medical expenses that Rickey required. By working two jobs, I was eventually able to buy a small business in Dallas. I needed the flexibility of self-employment so I could take off time to go to the school when necessary.

Disaster always seemed to be lurking around the corner. The people, who sold me the business, started another business outside Dallas and pulled all their old customers out from under me. I ended up having to close the doors.

Sometime later, God opened a door so that I was able to buy another small business. It was one of those miracles I had prayed for.

At the end of the school day, I could bring Rickey to work with me where he could play while I "kept the store." Due to the sale of the property where my business was located, I was forced to sell out. I had saved a little money which enabled me to take a few months off to be with Rickey full-time.

One day I walked into Rickey's classroom and, to my utter horror and disbelief, I saw the teacher knock Rickey to the floor! There was no debate. I checked Rickey out of that school quicker than most Texans move.

With no school for my son, I did not know what to do. He had to have a "special" school, but the good ones were scarce or too expensive. I prayed. Ultimately, with God's direction, and the support of Omagene Haft – a wonderful mother figure – I found a new school for Rickey.

We built our new home together which was only a few blocks from the school. It was another miracle, how God provided not only an exceptional teacher, but one who was also a Christian. Rickey's new school and new home made him feel secure, and gradually, he began to advance in his studies.

OLD PROBLEMS AND NEW MIRACLES

Among all the other physical problems that the doctor had warned me of when he gave me the first prognosis, was that this condition would stunt his growth. At regular checkups the doctor advised me to put Rickey on a special high protein diet; trusting it might enhance his physical growth. By this time, Rickey was about nine years old.

One day, Rickey came in, and out of the blue asked, "Can God make me grow taller?" I was a bit startled, but I answered, "Well, uh...yes, of course, son."

His eyes brightened really wide and he said, "Mother, tell God I want to be six feet tall!"

At that point, I felt that was a pretty "tall" order, but we began to pray everyday and anointing him with oil, according to the Word. As we continued in prayer regularly, Rickey began to grow normally, and of course the doctors were amazed.

God was blessing us in many ways and Rickey was progressing in many areas. One area I discovered through these trying years, was Rickey's dexterity; he was good with his hands.

As I thought on this, the Lord instructed me to teach Rickey three scriptures:

1. *As a man thinketh in his heart, so is he.* (paraphrase Philippians. 4:13)
2. *I can do all things through Christ.* (paraphrase 1 John 4:4)
3. *Greater is He that is in me than he that is in the world.* (paraphrase Proverbs 23:7)

As we were faithful to pray, work and confess the Word, Rickey developed at an astonishing rate, both physically and academically. Eventually, his instructors decided to start him on computers. His grades went from straight "F's" to straight "A's"!

"He sent his Word and healed them" (Psalms 107:20).

We learned throughout these hard years that God's Holy Word never fails to work when you appropriate it.

Though the days were hard on the one hand, it seemed like no time at all until Rickey was in high school.

One day, his high school teacher called to say he should be enrolled in a special school again. This time it was because they felt he was a "budding" genius on the computer.

Oh, how that thrilled us! God had not only brought Rickey through so many physical difficulties; He also worked a divine miracle!

My life had not been easy; still I had deep faith. I trusted God's Holy Spirit, always looking to Him for His solutions to my daily problems. It was God's intervention, which kept me going, and healed my child.

He has been my source since I was a young child looking up at the clouds speaking to him in the fields of Arkansas. Many times after that, in times of hardship, I sought him again asking "Is anybody up there?" He never failed to answer in His way.

Out of my deep love and gratitude to honor God for His gracious love, care, and keeping power through the years, I established The Rickey Lee Blasingame Foundation in 1979.

Rickey's foundation was, and is to this day, a foundation to help children who are mentally challenged and have special needs.

We were living in Mesquite, TX when the city had planned to have a parade. I called my brother, Hollis and I asked him to bring his truck so we could enter the parade. In only one hour, we decorated the truck and put in the parade. Cable TV carried the parade and gave us great publicity.

10

GOD…I'M AFRAID

In the midst of growing up, marriage, divorce, and life in general – the call of God was still on my life and in my heart to be in full time ministry. Things were difficult for me as a young, single mother with the sole responsibility of a child. I felt I could not step out in full-time ministry at this time.

About the time God was getting ready to put me UP in full-time ministry, I was thinking about going DOWN. Like Jonah, in the Old Testament, when God commanded him … "get up and go to Nineveh," Jonah was making plans to go DOWN to Joppa. I found that God always wins.

In 1980, I became disillusioned about a lot of things in my life, to the point that I became despondent. My biggest disappointment was my church. I even stopped going to church for a short while.

I loved God, but I couldn't handle "Christians" at that particular time in my life. I needed guidance and stability. I asked, "What do I do?"

One day, while I was meditating, I had a second experience with the Lord. My spirit left my body, and once again, I found myself back in Heaven very briefly. In loving mercy, He spoke to me.

"This time you are going to preach the gospel, and I am going to teach you how to walk in the power of the resurrection."

I felt I had waited too long to answer the call to preach, and I might not have the ability. (God called me in 1957, at age thirteen. It was now 1980.)

A few days later, a friend of mine handed me a book by the late Kathryn Kuhlman. I read it from cover to cover, engrossed, and wonderfully awed at what God could do through a life that was sold out to Him. One particular line greatly impressed me, **"God has done for me what He'll do for you if you will pay the price."**

I was now ready to serve the Master at any cost. I raised Ms. Kuhlman's book in my hand above my head and declared, "Jesus, whatever the price, I'm willing to pay it, if you will give me a ministry like hers plus a double portion."

The Lord took me seriously and He asked, "Do you mean what you say?"

"Yes, Lord."

By now, Rickey was fourteen years old. The Lord spoke to me one day and said, "You let Rickey go live with his father for eighteen months, and during that time I want you to go to your bedroom and fast and pray, and I will teach you how to follow the Holy Spirit."

This was a price I hadn't counted on. I didn't understand why God would ask this of me. To let my son leave was going to be difficult. How could I make Rickey understand what God was doing?

Within thirty minutes, Rickey came into my bedroom and said, "Mother, we need to have a mother and son talk."

We often had these one to one talks, so it wasn't unusual for Rickey to make such a request. I turned to him, anxious to hear what my tall son had to say. He got right to the point.

"Mother, I want to go live with my father for a year and a half."

I thought my heart would break, and yet, I knew only the Holy Spirit must have placed the desire and the exact length of time in Rickey's heart. Feeling sure that this was in God's will, I let Rickey go.

While Rickey was with his father, I spent eighteen to twenty hours a day reading the Word of God. I started at Genesis and ended at Revelation, and the Holy Spirit began to teach me how to interpret the Word.

Sometimes there would be a Scripture I didn't understand, but after spending a week reading it over and over again, God would reveal its meaning. It was a wonderful time of enlightenment.

I read in Luke's Gospel where Jesus fasted forty days. So, I went on four forty-day fasts during the eighteen months. After those eighteen months of prayer, fasting, and staying in the Word – I thought I was READY for the ministry! But the Charismatic Church was not ready for me.

I was unknown among the churches and pastors, and they were apprehensive about me. But, I was undaunted. If this was a test of my obedience to God who told me to pray for the sick, I was willing to pay the price.

I visited hospitals, introducing myself as a minister, then asking if I could visit patients in intensive care, especially those who were dying.

Most hospitals were cooperative. Sometimes I spent eight hours a day praying for patients, and God honored my dedication. Many of the patients for whom I prayed were healed, and encouraged.

I will never forget, one day I walked into a hospital and visited a lady who had been confined to the bed for forty-two days. She was now unable to walk, and the doctors could not find the reason for her illness. I greeted her warmly, and asked, "Is there some way I could help you? Would you like a magazine, or perhaps some candy?"

"No." She said. "What I really want is to get out of this bed!"

"Maybe we could pray," I suggested. She agreed, and I prayed.

After my prayer, she began to move her leg. I gently took her hands, and slowly, she got out of bed!

At that precise moment, her son-in-law, who was a doctor, walked into her room. He was astounded. He looked at his mother-in-law, and then he looked at me and asked in obvious amazement, "What happened?"

His mother-in-law began to tell him the story. And I explained it is a miracle of God. He said, "I don't understand all this, but you can come to this hospital and pray anytime you wish."

Later, that doctor began to support my ministry financially. And this is how my ministry of praying for the sick began to grow. My hospital work began to expand into the community as one, and then another, would tell about their healing. Soon, I was traveling to other cities outside of Dallas.

11

STEPPING OUT ON FAITH—THE BIGGEST STEP

One of the first meetings was in San Antonio, Texas. Only ten people came, but I was not discouraged. I knew if Jesus died to save just one soul, then it wouldn't be any problem for Him to heal these ten. God's Holy Spirit came and fell with healing power. One lady was healed of a blood disease, and a gentleman with a cast on his leg was gloriously healed. His cast broke and fell to the floor. The Lord was present to heal.

Even though there were only twelve, counting Rickey and me, that almost empty auditorium reverberated with praises to God, praises of delight and astonishment. The people were delighted and I was astonished!

During the meeting in San Antonio, God sent a couple who offered me the hospitality of their home. At the time, I was staying with my sister in San Antonio, and had no idea just how soon I would be grateful for their generous offer.

At this particular time, one of my brothers, Ron, came to visit us. When he found out what I was doing, he was very upset with me for preaching. In his mind, there was no such thing as a "lady evangelist," and Ron let me know in no uncertain terms that he was embarrassed and wanted no part of me or my preaching.

One night as I came home, my brother Ron met me at the door, yelling in an angry voice. "I am putting you, your clothes and your son's clothes out on the street!" Hurt and surprised by such treatment, I did not know what to do. I didn't have any money to return to Dallas, but my Heavenly Father God was quite aware of my circumstances.

As Rickey and I sat on the curb with earthly possessions, I was devastated. Not knowing what to do, I just bowed my head and cried. In the midst of my pain, the Lord spoke to me. He said, "I want you to fast for three days."

Then I remembered the couple who offered me their hospitality, and I called them one night after the meeting. It was only then that I learned my host couple were ministers. When I explained my predicament, they gave us a room in their garage where my son and I could sleep.

For those next three days, I fasted and prayed. And at the end of those three days, God said, "Boast not for what I will do tomorrow."

The following day my host's daughter came into the garage and asked me if I would go to the hospital with her. Her young daughter was totally paralyzed except for eye movement in right eyelid. They asked me to pray for her.

When we walked into the hospital room, it was obvious the grandchild was desperately ill. Without touching her, I simply put my hands above her head and asked God to let resurrection life flow through Dedra Ann Campbell.

Within three days, the child and her mother flew back to Panama to rejoin her father who served with the American Air Force. Shortly thereafter, I received the following letter from the child's mother:

> Dear Reverend Blasingame:
>
> Regarding the miracle that took place in Dedra Ann Campbell's life, age 12, I give you permission to use this miracle in any way to further the kingdom of God. And

also for the glory of God, that people may know God is the same "yesterday, today and forever," and that healing is for today.

Dedra sustained injuries from a playground accident on June 30, 1981. When she was admitted to the hospital that night, she was totally paralyzed in her extremities.

She was hospitalized from June 30, 1981 until September 4, 1981, and progressed each day until she walked out of the hospital on her own accord. She has regained full function of all extremities and was released from the hospital to resume normal activities.

We give God all the glory for her miracle healing and want to tell the whole world. I am attaching Dedra's doctor's Clinical Records.

In Christian Love,

Clifteen Campbell

MIRACLES IN COLORADO

After San Antonio, I was praying for direction for the next meeting when the Lord gave me a vision, and in the vision, He told me to go to Colorado. The vision was simply of a painting with four flowers.

This is strange, I thought, since I didn't know anyone in Colorado, but God told me to go, and I knew if I obeyed, and started to Colorado, God would direct me.

Rickey was traveling with me, and when we got all packed and headed for Colorado, I told him that when I get to a place with a picture of four flowers, I would know we are at the right place. He looked at me sort of funny, but he also knew that I obeyed God, even when it didn't make sense.

The Holy Spirit directed me to exit. I pulled off the highway and drove down the street and into a church parking lot. The only thing I knew to do at this point was to go in and find the pastor.

Inside the church, I found the pastor's secretary outside his office. I introduced myself, and she called for the pastor. He was a kindly, middle-aged man.

"Hello," I said. "My name is Loretta Blasingame. I'm an evangelist, and God told me to come to Colorado." A curious slight smile slipped across the pastor's face, and he asked, "Are you from Texas?"

"Yes, I am," I said with mild surprise, "how did you know?"

"Well," he smiled again, "God told me he was sending me a minister from Texas."

Now, I was really surprised. Even though God told me to go to Colorado, I was stunned at his words. Momentarily, I couldn't believe God had already prepared him for my coming.

Politely ignoring my stunned silence, he continued, "I prayed, asking God to send me a minister because I really needed to be away for awhile." His answer to me was, "I am sending you a minister from Texas." However, he was smiling, "He failed to mention that the minister He would send would be a woman."

We both laughed, and then, very seriously, he said, "I need someone to fill in for me for the next two and a half months — could you do that for me?" I think I stuttered and couldn't seem to find the words when his secretary stepped in and graciously offered us accommodations. She explained, "I'm going to Denver to a seminar, and you and your son are welcome to stay at my ranch."

This was almost too much, but finally I found the words to agree to take the church for the two and a half month period. And soon, the secretary, my son and I were on the way to her ranch home.

When she opened the door to her lovely home, and we were all inside, the first thing that met my gaze was a beautiful painting of four gorgeous flowers. It was the one the Lord showed me in the vision before I left Dallas. I knew beyond all doubt that I was where I was supposed to be.

During those two and a half months, serving as pastor/ evangelist, I conducted a number of healing services, and the Lord moved mightily.

I will always remember a young lady named Cindy who had been paralyzed due to an accidental shooting incident. Her father flew to Dallas, picked her up and flew her to Colorado to bring her to the church. While I was preaching the Lord said to me, "Ask Cindy if she loves you."

I thought to myself, *that is a strange thing to say,* but I looked at Cindy and asked her, "Cindy, do you love me?"

"Loretta, you know I do," she said sincerely. I said "In the name of Jesus, just get out of that wheelchair and come hug my neck." "No, Cindy, don't move," her father shouted, fearing she might fall. She said, "But, I love Loretta, and I want to hug her neck." Her father came closer to help her, and slowly, she rose out of the wheelchair, totally healed. I didn't even pray. She simply came and hugged my neck, and Jesus healed her.

During the first two weeks in Colorado, there were many miraculous healings of cancer which doctors later verified. Most of them were healed as I was preaching. The miracles were great, and the word began to spread. This is what can happen when God's people walk in obedience.

12

GUIDED BY FAITH

Following the Colorado mission, we returned to Dallas. Shortly thereafter, I went with two other ladies to Jerusalem. There I met a lady living in Jerusalem, who had sung with Kathryn Kuhlman's choir. She asked me if I would drive with her to Los Angeles, California when we returned to the U.S.

Not long after we returned home, she called to say she was ready to go to Los Angeles, so I invited her to come to Dallas. And from Dallas, we drove to Los Angeles.

No sooner had we arrived in Los Angeles, Rickey said he wanted to meet Dr. Rolf McPherson, son of Sister Aimee McPherson, Founder of The Four Square Denomination and Angelus Temple. Rickey had heard me tell how Dr. McPherson, after the untimely death of his mother, carried on her ministry.

I had told Rickey how much Rolf loved his mother and how he stood by Sister Aimee all those years. Rickey was obviously impressed and he said he wanted to be just like Rolf McPherson. So he began telling his friends that he was going to have a meeting with Dr. McPherson to ask him to pray over him.

Rickey said that he wanted to be to me what Rolf had been to his mother. They scoffed at his notion, saying Dr. McPherson was too busy to see him. But Rickey said, "I have prayed, and God told me Dr. McPherson will see me."

After arriving, one of the first things we did was take Rickey to Dr. McPherson's office. I explained to Dr. Leita May Stewart, the secretary, why we were there, praying under my breath at the same time.

Dr. Stewart was very gracious, and said, since we did not have an appointment, a meeting was unlikely, but to wait there. Rickey looked at me and said, "Don't worry, mother, he's a man of God. God will tell him to see me."

The door swung open and with a big smile Ms. Stewart announced, "Mr. Blasingame, you may go in."

Rickey's face beamed, "Mother, you wait here." So, I waited, and as I waited, I prayed, and wondered what was taking place inside that office.

Forty-five minutes later, my son came out of Dr. McPherson's office and announced. "I know everything I need to know, mother. I'm going to stand with you just like Rolf stood with his mother."

So Rickey had his day. Later, he told his friends in detail about his forty-five minutes with Dr. Rolf McPherson—a man of God. They stood in wide-eyed amazement.

Loretta and Rickey praying together in 1983.

THE HOLY SPIRIT'S LEADING THROUGH THE FGBFI

While we were still in Los Angeles, the Holy Spirit spoke to me and told me to go to the Full Gospel Business Men's Fellowship International Convention. I didn't know why He wanted me to go to a Businessmen's Convention, but I obeyed.

I entered by the front door, and not knowing what to do, I just stood still, and I asked the Holy Spirit, "What do I do now and where do I go?"

He said, **"See that escalator in front of you—get on it and ride to the top. Get off and just stand there."** I obeyed.

As I stepped off the escalator, a man briskly walked up to me and said, "Come, go with me. I want to talk to you. I know you have seen Jesus, and I want you to tell me about it."

Behind him were two TV cameras and a sofa. He invited me to sit down and then turned to a young man whom I later learned was his son, and said "I know this woman has seen Jesus. I can tell by the shine on her face."

I was a bit shocked when he told his son to turn on both of the TV cameras and keep them rolling. As far as I know, he had no way of knowing me and I certainly did not know him. He had no idea what the Holy Spirit had in store for him.

He opened the "interview," and as I began to talk about my trip to Heaven, he began to cry right there in front of the camera and everyone. To the cameras he said, "I told you this woman has seen Jesus!"

I was so surprised that this man, whom I had never met, had just put me on video. He had the kindest heart and such a love for God. When we finished, he thanked me for sharing my experience, and asked, "What is your name?"

It seemed like the cart before the horse, but I answered, "My name is Loretta Blasingame, I have never been on TV, so I'm sure you haven't ever heard of me." "No, I haven't and I'm sorry for that. I have been missing out." He smiled. "I have extensive TV exposure in Mexico right now, and with your permission, I would like to air this tape."

I felt honored, and consented. Not long afterward, I received a call from a lady in Oklahoma who had just seen my tape which a man in Mexico had sent her. For several years, people in many places would call me and tell me they had seen that video.

The Holy Spirit said:

"Where does the scripture cometh, neither from the East, nor from the West, nor from the South. But God is the judge; He putteth down one and setteth up another" (Paraphrase of Psalm 75:6-7).

Remember? I did say I had "stepped out in faith."

The Holy Spirit knows how to promote for the Kingdom of God. This "incidental meeting" certainly promoted our ministry on the West Coast.

Shortly thereafter, we moved to San Diego, California and rented a facility where I started a Bible School and taught people how to follow the leading of the Holy Spirit.

I stressed to the students that we must be guided by the Holy Spirit – not tell the Holy Spirit what we are going to do. I continued my teaching and also conducted healing services in rented halls.

Seven years before, the Lord had given me a vision of a piece of property in Oceanside, California and even the name of it during one of my forty day fasts. (I have actually fasted for forty days on four occasions.)

In the vision, He showed me the ocean and told me to buy the property. The Lord also told me it would be seven years later before I would buy the property.

Seven years rolled by and I contacted the owner and asked him how much he wanted for the property. He indicated that he did not want to sell now. So I made him another offer and told him to call if he changed his mind. Then, I said to the Lord, “If he doesn’t call me within twenty-four hours and take my offer, I will release this.”

The next day I was at a radio station making tapes when the owner of the property called and said, “I’ll sell the property, but it will cost $1.5 million dollars!”

I called my real estate man to go with me. The Holy Spirit had given me a word that **“I was to hold my own with this man.”** I thought, *God, that’s a strange word. You know I am a meek person. What does that mean?*

At his home, the owner said, “I want $350,000 down.” “No,” I firmly replied. “A hundred and fifty thousand,” he countered. “No,” I said again. He was beginning to raise his voice at me.

I said, “Don’t try to intimidate me, and don’t raise your voice at me. You can have the twenty dollars I have.” (That was all I had.)

When I said that, he stood up, and looking shocked at my holy boldness said, “I like you, you’ve, got guts. No one has ever stood up to me before. I’ve got six people now waiting to buy this property; but you can have it for $1.5 million. You can move in tomorrow.”

I was somewhat taken aback at his referring to me as “The Lady with guts…” but I received the property with nothing down. The Lord brought me a million dollar miracle.

The Scripture says, You shall buy without money:

> *"Ho, every one that thirsteth, come ye to the waters, and he that hath no money; come ye, buy, and eat; yea, come, buy wine and milk without money and without price. Wherefore do ye spend money for that which is not bread? And your labor for that which satisfieth not! Hearken diligently unto me, and eat ye that which is good, and let your soul delight itself in fatness" (Isaiah 55:1-2).*

1640 Northgate - purchased by God in 24 hours.

We moved into this property and started a Bible School for young people. Some had been put out of their homes. God later restored them through our ministry. Many of the young people gave their hearts to the Lord, and together with this small group, we prayed about starting a church. Today they all have good jobs.

STILL SUNNY IN CALIFORNIA

My brother, Otis, the brother who took me to church at age 13 when I was saved, wrote me a letter saying that in a couple of months he was going to retire.

He also said that he would come to California to help me build the Church. God was moving on our prayers. I looked forward to his help in our undertaking.

In the meantime, Reverend Cliff Orndorf and his family were to hold a tent meeting with another evangelist. The day the meeting was to start, the evangelist was assaulted.

Reverend Orndorf asked me to do the meetings in his place. The meetings lasted two weeks. God was really moving, and at the end of the two weeks, on a Sunday, I started my church in the home of Dr. J.C. and Virginia Fikes.

After the service that Sunday, everyone, including my board members, made a circle around me to pray. My mind had a lot of thoughts running through it. I felt they didn't like the way I preached, or didn't think I made a good pastor. And as they encircled me, I thought, *They should at least give me a chance.* It was my first message as a pastor, and I expected a little compassion.

Soon, I discovered the real reason for their circle of prayer.

Dr. Fikes had received a call from Dallas that my brother, Otis, had a heart attack and died. They were praying to God to sustain me and comfort me.

I was speechless for a moment. I could not understand how this could have happened. My brother had never had heart trouble. His twin brother, Hollis, had a couple of heart attacks resulting in heart surgery. I could have understood if it had been him. I wrote Otis two weeks before to tell him how much I loved him for fasting and praying me into the Kingdom.

Since Otis was responsible for me being a Christian, my family felt I should preach his funeral service. At the time, I felt I could not possibly do it, but again, I simply put my faith in God, and I found His strength was sufficient to see me through. I was soon to see how God closed one door only to open another.

On July 12, 1985, I was speaking at a Full Gospel Business Men's Fellowship breakfast meeting. Near the close of the meeting, Joe Klinsinger, President of the Chapter, started to lead my brother Ron in the prayer of salvation, but he said, "No. My sister Loretta will lead me to the Lord. She believed God to save me when all the time I said no. I even put her out on the street at one time."

Ron gave his heart to the Lord that morning as I issued the invitation for salvation. What a joyful day that was for me! It was in July of 1980 that God told me the month and the day Ron would come into the Kingdom.

That very day Ron was delivered from drugs and alcohol without withdrawals. I thank God for the calling of the Full Gospel Business Men's Fellowship International, and for saving my brother.

In 1980, God gave me a vision that, in due season, my brother would join me in the ministry. I thank God for how He fulfilled that vision. Ron was with me when Otis went home to be with the Lord.

At that same meeting, I gave my testimony about my trip to Heaven. As a result, there were so many miracles; I spoke at the Los Angeles Chapter three months in a row. I specifically remember speaking for the Orange County Chapter where God blessed us with many mighty miracles of healing and salvation.

At the same meeting, I was introduced to Dick Mills who received a great word from the Lord about my ministry. Dick was on the same program and spoke before I did. When he finished, he told the men about my faith, and encouraged every one of them to stay for the service that I was conducting afterward.

Demos Shakarian, the late Founder and President of the Full Gospel Business Men's Fellowship International, told all the chapter presidents to open their meetings to me. These meetings with FGBMFI, as you have been reading, launched my ministry in California.

In 1993, I spoke to the Eastern Regional Convention at Pat Robertson's Founder's Inn in Virginia Beach and then held a healing service. Principal convention speakers were Demos Shakarian, Pat Robinson, Paul Walker, Dick Mills and Rear Admiral Grady Jackson, U.S.N.

On Brother Shakarian's endorsement, I was also booked to speak at a FGBMFI meeting in the Grand Cayman Islands. I was privileged to be on the same program with Sir Lionel Luckhoo.

At a later date, the FGBMFI booked me to speak for ten days in Wellington, New Zealand where we saw God moving mightily to save and heal. I will always be grateful to the FGBMFI Chapters, and Brother Shakarian who so graciously supported my ministry.

Visit of Pastor Blasingame to New Zealand in 1994

When Pastor Blasingame was having a series of meetings with the Full Gospel Businessmen's Fellowship Wellington Chapter in 1994, they used our church building.

I and some of my church people attended and we were very blessed under her ministry. Particularly her testimony was wonderful. I shared a little bit of her testimony with the Korean Ambassador, who wasn't a believer, and he and his wife (a Christian) became very curious to meet her. They invited Ps Blasingame for lunch and were both deeply impressed.

Several of my church attendees received the baptism of the Holy Spirit with speaking in tongues under her ministry. It was encouraging for me and edifying for my church. Since I am a woman pastor, it was wonderful to see God using her to bless many people around the world.

May god bless her and her ministry.

Pastor Kim Sook Claasen
Wellington Full Gospel Church

Wellington Full Gospel Church, Pastor Kim Sook Claasen ministered on August 21, 1994 with Loretta Blasingame.

DEATH TAKES NO HOLIDAYS

The Lord told me a curious thing even before Ron came to California. He said that Ron would come to me because he was dying, but he would be saved and would be with me for a season.

Death was working in Ron's body when he came; he was dying from hepatitis of the liver. The doctors gave us little hope that Ron would live.

I began to teach Ron the Word, and how to pray. I worked with him for several hours a day every day, and he was with me from 1985 to 1989. I thank God that I could provide a place for him to stay and take care of his needs.

The miracle is, that Ron was one of my brothers. The one who disowned me and threw me out of my sister's house in San Antonio, Texas because I was preaching the gospel. He even told people that I was dead. But thank God, Ron was saved through my ministry before he died.

Finally, Ron was hospitalized and lay in a coma, but each time I came to visit him, he would come out of the coma and talk with me. On one of those days, Ron said, "Loretta, you will have to go on alone from here. I don't want you to pray anymore for me to live. It's time for me to go home. To stay would only be a hindrance to your ministry."

I could not keep the tears back. Ron and I were very close and my heart broke. How could I make it without Ron? He was my friend and my brother. I enjoyed the times I sat at the hospital and read the Word of God to him. I had promised Ron I would be with him when the Lord took him home.

Sometimes, I walked into his room and tears would run down my cheeks unhidden. Ron would see me and say, "Loretta, you are too brave to cry. Go get a cup of coffee."

The night the Lord took Ron home, he asked me to pray, and as I did, I looked at his face. There was a heavenly glow on his face, and then he slipped into the arms of Jesus.

All of my family was in Dallas, and I was in Oceanside, California. I felt alone at first, but Jesus walked with me; I felt His presence. Even ministers feel empty and alone when there is a death—until God, the Holy Spirit and Comforter comes.

God sent a very good friend of Ron's, Dan Jordinelli, to help me with arrangements at the funeral home, and to take Ron's body back to Dallas. I knew the trip would be difficult, and soon I found myself walking through the valley of death again as the plane soared through the clouds transporting my brother's body back to Dallas.

I will forever be grateful to our friend Dan Jordinelli for flying with me on this long, weary trip, and being such a comfort.

The thought of Ron's lifeless body in the baggage room of the plane brought tears again to my eyes. But my comfort came as I quoted the 23rd Psalm under my breath.

I could feel God's love and mercy flowing toward us. I remembered the scripture, "Love never faileth." His love never left me. Jesus again was the Author of my Faith.

Since then, there have been many trials and tribulations, but God has been faithful. There has never been a trial that God failed to carry me through. However, unknown to me, my greatest challenge was still to come.

13

THE CHALLENGE OF MY LIFE

A friend and I had gone out for lunch. When I arrived home, I saw a large note on my car. It read:

"Jeanne, don't leave. Make sure you come into the house with Loretta." I knew something was wrong. I jumped out of the car and ran inside.

My friend, Omagene, and I had built a house together so we could have Rickey in the school close by. Omagene was a spiritual mother to me.

When I opened the door, Omagene stood crying uncontrollably, and through her tears she managed to say: "Rickey is dead!"

I glanced at her and said, "What a terrible thing to say!"

Through her crying voice she said, "The police called your mother and told her that Rickey was found dead early this morning in his car in Palmer, Texas." (A little town outside of Dallas.)

I was numb. All I could hear was someone screaming. Time stood still. I don't know how long it was when I realized the screaming was me. I was screaming things like, "It's not so—someone has made a mistake. This couldn't happen."

Before my friend Jeanne drove me to my mother's house, I told her I needed a moment alone. I fell on my knees and cried out to God. I sobbed, "Oh, God tell me something that will carry me through this. I don't want to fall apart… ."

I thought I would not be able to stand this—I felt as though my heart was being ripped out of me.

Then suddenly, The Lord said: ***"Lean not on your own understanding but trust in the Lord."***

There was a crowd of people—then I could see faces: My favorite Uncle Terrell, my mother was standing close, crying so hard she couldn't talk. I couldn't see or talk for the tears, but suddenly I felt more compassion for my mother than myself.

All my family was around me, and I thanked God for them and for the Holy Spirit who was sent to heal the broken-hearted. They seemed to know exactly what to do--but I was numb. I just sat there with my mind going in a hundred different directions.

How did this happen? Is he really dead? Who did this? Is this a dream? What am I going to do?

There were no answers to anything. My family was doing all they could to help but, they were as devastated as I was. It was like time stood still.

Someone took care of the family and the crowd that had gathered. Jeanne took me to a quieter place while the others tried to bring order out of chaos.

My dear closest friends stood silently by. No words could describe the scene. Only low sobs. I waited for the Lord to comfort my heart and bring comfort to my spirit.

It could have been a scene from the Old Testament of Job. Time had no meaning, but after what seemed a millennium, a thought came to my spirit. Vague as it was, it slowly came into focus. I began to remember the last visit Rickey and I had together.

I guess *"the how's"* were the biggest question. Then the thought came into view – the visit Rickey and I had. It was only a week before his death.

I was in my office at the house when Rickey came bouncing through the door – first stop, kitchen, got a cold drink, poured a coke and came into my office. Plopping down in a chair, and stretching his long legs under my desk, he said, "Mother, I couldn't sleep last night, so I just prayed for you until somewhere around 4:00 a.m."

"During that time, the Lord gave me a vision of your ministry. He showed me several very large buildings full of people. There were people standing outside as well. The Lord told me to look at the buildings. He said, 'The buildings will never be big enough to hold the crowds.'And in the midst of this good-sounding news, He said, 'Tell your mother not to be discouraged and to never give up.'"

Switching his position and looking far away, he continued, "I saw a television screen with your name being flashed across it. On the screen it gave your name, the name of a building and dates of your crusades. Then the Lord repeated, 'Tell your mother never to be discouraged and never to give up.'"

I chuckled and said, "Son, have you ever known your mother to give up?"

"No, Mother, and I don't know why Jesus told me to tell you not to give up."

Then, another brief silence, and Rickey asked if he could see the beginning notes on the book I had began, and for the prayer requests from my radio broadcast. I said: "Do you mean the one from KSKY here in Dallas?" He said, "Yes."

So, I gathered them from a drawer, and he laid his hands on the requests and the unfinished manuscript. And Rickey said, "God, please answer the prayer requests from the radio broadcast," and lifting my unfinished book, he continued, "and God, please publish Mother's book and make it a No. 1 bestseller."

Then Rickey laid his hand on my shoulder and lifting his head toward Heaven said, "Father, I also ask you to send enough angels from Heaven to fulfill everything you have shown me in the vision."

After his prayer for me, he asked me to pray, so I laid hands on him and offered a prayer up to the Throne Room of Heaven, thanking God for my only son.

I was greatly encouraged by this beautiful vision, and I could tell that Rickey was pleased, but his next statement added a sad and dubious note to our conversation. He said very seriously, "Mother, if I am ever found dead, even with a suicide note, don't believe it."

Rickey always did have a way with the "shock" factor. This certainly shocked my inner being – these words just didn't make sense to me. There were a million questions I wanted to ask him, but he had already shifted to this world of his own that most young people seem to live in. So I just tried to shrug off my feeling by saying, "Well, don't worry Rickey, nothing like that will ever happen to you."

That was the last meaningful talk we shared. Only one week later tragedy struck, and Rickey was found dead. His death has never been solved; there are mysteries that still surround his death. Only God knows what happened.

Again, as in the past, my heart went back to that day in a beautiful green field in Arkansas when God revealed His reality to my young heart. I was only four years old, but I knew and understood that there was a God and He was real, and I could talk to Him and He would answer.

I could not explain it as a child or theologian – but I have never doubted it and He has never failed to prove Himself as my divine Father and Helper. Every tragedy or blessing in my life since that time has manifested His care and Presence.

So standing there amid my loving family, I decided again, as always, to give my broken heart to the Lord. Moreover, I have decided to continue to trust Him as the Lord of my life. Furthermore, I decided to continue the ministry to which He called me.

I will hold on to that last meaningful conversation with Rickey, and I will do what God has called me to do and to trust Him to take care of what I can't.

Briefly, these are the words God burned deep into my spirit that day in a green Arkansas field – the field became mysteriously quiet – even the live stock stood quiet and motionless "IS ANYBODY UP THERE?" And like a streak of lightening the words flashed across my heart: He said**, *"I AM GOD…I AM HERE!"***

My purpose now is to do what the Lord gave my son in the vision a week before his death — to never give up — and to fulfill the vision depending solely on the Holy Spirit.

Loretta and Rickey in 1989.

14

MY MOTHER'S LAST WORDS ON HER HOMEGOING

I was conducting meetings in California and had been there quite some time when I got a phone call from one of my sisters in Dallas. She said that mother was critically ill, and the doctors said she could possibly die.

I packed my car that night and got up early the next morning and drove straight through to Dallas.

When I arrived at my mother's home, she began to talk to me immediately. She said, "I am very tired, but I have had one of the best lives of anybody. I do not want you to pray for the Lord to heal me this time because I am tired – my body is tired and I just want to go to heaven."

During the time that I stayed there, mother did go into the hospital. While she was in one of the hospital's doing rehab, her heart literally stopped, but the doctor's were able to revive her. Then, she was taken to another hospital.

It was very interesting what had happened to mother during her hospital stay. She said she took a quick little trip into heaven.

When she told me this, for a moment, I had flashbacks of when the Lord took me by the right hand into the throne room of heaven.

She went on to say that the Lord told her to pray over me. My mother always seemed to do everything right, but she never had prayed over me audibly. When I would pray, I would always say "God, please let my mother pray with me before you take her to heaven."

Back in my mother's hospital room, she told me that the Lord told her to take my right hand and put it over my left hand and to pray over me. And then He said to her: "Tell Loretta wherever she goes, whether she decides to stay and live in Dallas — it's alright. Whether she decides to go back to California or anywhere else — wherever she goes, tell Loretta that I have always taken care of her, I have always blessed her. Tell her that I will always go with her wherever she goes, and I will always take care of her. Tell her not to worry — right now she is worrying."

What my mother didn't know was that I, too, was having a few health challenges. But, I was trusting in the Lord and standing in faith. I hadn't told anyone. I guess there were times when fear would come in, and maybe I was worrying, but I didn't realize it was worrying.

However, this is what the Lord had told my mother. "Tell Loretta to stop worrying. She has nothing to worry about — I will always take care of her wherever she goes."

I thought it was quite amazing how the Lord spoke to her since she was not a church going person as we were growing up.

As the time drew near for the Lord to take my mother, God spoke to me one day and said, "In four days, I will take your mother to heaven — I will take her at 4:00 am in the morning."

I had gone over to my mother's home because she had left the hospital and wanted to be at home. So, they brought her to the house so she could go home to be with the Lord from there.

It was Saturday, and mother had asked all the children (that were still living, nine of us), to come over to the house. We had the best time with her. She even had us to straighten up all of the family pictures on the wall. Then, she told my brother to vacuum the house. She actually told all of us she was going home to heaven that night.

When she said it, my family looked at her and smiled. My brother Wallace said to me "Do you think mother is okay — she's not going to heaven is she?" I said, "Wallace, I do believe that mother is hearing from the Lord."

The next morning, we laughed and visited while Wallace was fixing breakfast for mother. Suddenly she said "Go and tell Wallace to set the breakfast off of the burner and come in here, I have something very important I need to tell him."

So, I returned to the kitchen and gave him mother's message. He laughed and said "well, the gravy will probably have lumps, but I will."

Wallace set the gravy off of the burner, and my mother was laughing and seemingly feeling good.

As we were laughing, I reached over on the table where there was a small piece of paper. I gave it to her, and she said, "Oh I have been wondering where that was."

When my brother and the rest of the family gathered at her bedside, she took the piece of paper and said, "Set down I want to do something."

The piece of paper had the lyrics to an old southern country and western song Tennessee Waltz. Now, to my knowledge, my mother had never sung a day in her life. She took the paper with the words and sang it to all of us.

Then, she looked at my brother Wallace and said:

> Now in the morning, when I go to heaven, I do not want to hear any crying going on because I will be in heaven. The Lord has helped me to take care of all of you.

But, the Lord will come down here and will take care of you Himself. I will be with the good Lord up above, and I don't want any crying. I don't want anybody carrying on — I don't want to hear about any grief going on.

And, every time you want to cry, I want you to think about how funny this was today that I stopped breakfast and sang one of my old favorite southern songs for all of you.

I want all of you to know that you all have made me the happiest mother that has ever lived on earth. And I want you all to remain happy.

Those were our mother's dying words. Her entire life made us all very happy, and she wanted to see that we would continue to serve the Lord and remain a happy family. What a lady!

Mother (Justine), still full of life at the age of 91.

PART TWO

Miracles of Healing and Deliverance

DOCTORS SAY "LITTLE JOEY HAS 30 PERCENT CHANCE TO SURVIVE CANCER SURGERY"

As told to Evangelist Loretta Blasingame by
Mr. & Mrs. Art Peterson
Parents of Little Joey

The day I walked into Little Joey's hospital room I saw a beautiful eighteen-month-old blonde headed boy – dying with cancer. I had been advised of the prognosis earlier. The doctor said there was only a thirty per cent chance that he would survive surgery. I hate to admit it, but when I saw him, he looked to me like he would soon be dead.

I had flown to Minneapolis, Minnesota to conduct a healing crusade for Reverend L.D. Kramer. However, when I arrived, he asked me if I would consent to go to the hospital to pray for Little Joey who was dying with cancer. So here I stood in Little Joey's hospital room. When I saw his frail little body, I wondered, Do I have the faith for this? Then, suddenly, before I could be plagued with more doubt, the Holy Spirit filled my entire being. Faith took over and Fear vanished. I prayed for Little Joey's complete healing in the mighty Name of Jesus. We left him with a blessing. I went on to my crusade.

A couple of month later, I'm sitting in the same church where I'd come to conduct a healing crusade when suddenly a little bundle of energy comes running down the aisle, jumps up in my lap and asked very excitedly: "Do you know who I am?

No one had told me that Little Joey would be at the church meeting or anything. I looked at him, and I said, "Well, no, I guess I don't know who you are."

At that, he put his little hand on his side and he said: "Well, I'm Little Joey!" My mouth flew open and he continued: "Do you see me? I'm Little Joey! I'm alive and you know what? I'm going to live a long, long time!"

Need I tell you how the rest of the meeting went that night? It was glorious.

I want to share with you the details of the glorious story of Little Joey's miracle healing of cancer. My good friends, Mr. and Mrs. Art Peterson, Little Joey's parents tell the story together.

Is Anybody Up There?

<u>Art:</u> We were living in Savage Minnesota. Joey seemed to be a perfectly normal little boy. He was about eighteen months old. One day he started wheezing a little and we didn't know what it was. It didn't get any better. If anything it was getting worse.

The wheezing seemed to be coming from his nose or lungs. We really couldn't be sure. But Claudia, my wife, who is a registered nurse said, "We are taking him to the doctor."

<u>Claudia:</u> By the time we got to the doctor's office, Little Joey was hardly wheezing at all. The doctor's nurse looked Little Joey over and kinda petted him on the head and said, "Oh, he's just fine and he looks so good. They were about to let us go back home.

About the time, the doctor poked his head in the door and said, "Did you get an x-ray?"

The nurse asked in a questioning way, "Well why would I need to do that?" But we all know one doesn't question the doctor. So she took him for the x-ray. The x-ray showed a large mass on Little Joey's right lung.

After seeing the mass, the doctor said "We need to get Little Joey to The Minnesota Children's Hospital right away."

We couldn't believe it – we were almost in shock.

After all the preliminaries at the Children's hospital they decided on surgery. First, they did an MRI and a CATSCAN to get the size of the mass and then performed surgery a couple of days later.

<u>Art:</u> After the surgery. The doctors came in and told us they got the tumor. It was cancerous and that they would have to begin chemotherapy as soon as possible. Claudia and I just felt numb. We just didn't expect anything like this.

When they initially diagnosed Little Joey with cancer, the first surgery was to remove the mass that was in his chest. The mass was compared to the size of a football. They took samples of the mass and came back telling us that it was lung cancer or a tumor, and that after surgery, Little Joey would have to go through weeks of chemotherapy.

<u>Claudia:</u> As the doctor talked, I broke down, I was crying. I was hearing words they were saying, but not really hearing. The doctor said, "do you want me to stop?" I said, "no, keep going. But really, all I was hearing was CANCER.

Doctors Say Little Joey has...

The diagnosis of cancer and chemotherapy, and all its ramifications, and the thought of death to our baby son was just the worst thing that could ever happen. We knew right then we were to look to God for our hope.

Little Joey was in surgery for three hours. The doctor said it was a difficult surgery because when he touched the tumor it crumpled in his hand and kind of disintegrated. I felt that this was Jesus doing the healing by making it a lot smaller. Along with the disintegration, Little Joey had lost a lot of blood.

Later one of the doctors took me outside and said, "Mrs. Peterson, I'm very sorry, but I'm afraid that Little Joey has only a 30 percent chance of recovery."

I just went numb and trembling. I sort of mumbled, 'O.K,' or something like that. But deep in my spirit faith was being kindled, and in spite of it all, I felt that Little Joey was being healed. My mind went back to before the children were born. I'd had a physical problem which included infertility and yet, God had given us two beautiful children. I didn't feel that God would bless me with two children and then take one away. So, I stood firm that this was an attack from the devil and he would not get away with it.

They did the surgery on a Friday and the following Tuesday; they started the chemotherapy. This was the beginning of a long ordeal that turned out to be long and tiresome trips of going to the hospital for three weeks and then back home for three weeks. I was one hundred percent positive that our church would be lifting us up in prayer. Then one day during this time, Reverend Kramer and Evangelist Loretta Blasingame came to the hospital and prayed for Little Joey. I knew all along in my spirit that Little Joey was being healed.

We sincerely thank God and the surgical team. They had to establish what kind of cancer it was. After that, they had to administer chemotherapy. This went on for about six months. Little Joey made it through but it was a long, tedious journey. Our lives consisted of taking Little Joey to the hospital for three weeks' treatment and back home for three weeks.

During this time we learned that when anyone has chemotherapy they lose their immune system and they are not able to fight off infection. But it turned out that Little Joey had "zero" infections the whole time. He went for one year just as healthy as a chemotherapy patient could be.

<u>Art:</u> Then after about six months they were pretty sure that the cancer was gone. However after looking at the first surgery again, the doctors

discovered some spots on Little Joey's ribs where the first cancer had started. They felt it would be best to take out those two ribs. This meant another year of hospital, chemotherapy, and all that goes with this type of surgery.

They alternated the times and the different types of chemotherapy for one year. We were at the hospital most of the time – constantly going back and forth for chemotherapy treatments.

Claudia: I believe they were making sure that the lungs were clear. We learned that sometimes after surgery one can develop pneumonia which is very serious. A cancer patient is not able to fight off the various kinds of infections. They were going to start giving him special treatments. In the meantime, the nurse had just come in and she had finished up the first special treatment. Shortly after that, the doctor peeks in the door and says "never mind he's okay." And that was a definite miracle!

Art: We never felt angry with God. We just put our trust in him and hung on to His word: "...by His stripes we are healed" (Isaiah 53:5).

Claudia: It was a tough road for that year, but we did have a peace and a deep faith. Little Joey was a real little hero; he withstood all the obstacles of pneumonia and the various blood defects that can happen. He is a survivor. God made him whole and stronger than ever. He is the toughest little seven-year old you could imagine. He is proud of his scars and wears them proudly -- 'proud' that God healed him.

This experience has brought us much closer as a family – and a great deal closer to the Lord. We thank Him and praise Him every day for healing Little Joey. His experience has brought us from being an everyday "normal family" with "normal" kids to a wonderful little guy who has been healed of cancer by a wonderful group of nurses, doctors and our glorious Lord Jesus.

I would like to repeat the importance of believing the Word of God: "…by His stripes we are healed" (Isaiah 53:5). Claudia and I claim that Word for our family everyday. I would just encourage everyone to read the Word of God, and if you or a loved one needs healing, to seek out a Scriptural healing ministry like Evangelist Loretta Blasingame. The proof is right here in Little Joey's life: "by His stripes we are healed." We just continue to thank God everyday.

Claudia: I believe in miracles – miracles are for everyone. We are a normal, regular family, but we have experienced the ultimate of gifts–and that is the miracle of God's gift–glorious life!

As a humble part of Little Joey's miracle of healing I want to say that today, six years later, Little Joey is still healed and is still a healthy young school boy. He enjoys playing the violin with his big brother, Jeremiah, as well as doing all the things two healthy boys like to do, playing football, riding their bikes and especially playing their instruments together. I want you to know, He can heal you, too.

The Peterson's - enjoying a family outing together.

Claudia and Joey's older brother Jeremiah, and Art and "Little Joey".

Claudia and "Little Joey" enjoying their miracle of healing.

GOD'S METHOD OF HEALING IS PERFECT

Testimony of Healing from Breast Cancer

In June of 1981, I felt pain in my left breast. At first I ignored it, but the pain increased. It was not a sharp pain, but a deep, penetrating, sickening pain that is hard to describe. Once before that time, I had felt the same kind of pain in a different part of my body, which proved to be a very serious condition that was later healed miraculously through prayer in the name of Jesus.

Immediately, I prayed that the Lord would show me where to go for prayer. By that time, I wanted to go directly to Him to be healed because I knew that His methods of healing are perfect. One night as I prayed and cried out to Jesus, I felt anxious and concerned. For a number of years, I had kept in touch with Oral Roberts Ministry, and I asked the Lord, "How can I possibly get to Oral Roberts for prayer? I don't have the energy to travel, and I need to keep working because I have very little money." A soft voice spoke inside my head, saying, "Well, Loretta Blasingame is at Old Pisgah just a short distance away. Why don't you go there for her to pray for you?"

About a month before that time, I had met Loretta Blasingame when I had visited Ruth Selway, a friend at Old Pisgah; and she had prayed with me concerning a financial matter. Immediately, I called Loretta to ask if she was having a special healing service, but I said nothing about my condition. She told me that she would be ministering with Laete Thomas that Saturday evening. I was there.

When Loretta and Laete Thomas asked people to come forward who needed healing, I was one of the first at the altar. Both ladies started to pray for me. After a short time Loretta walked closer to me and whispered in my ear so that I would not be embarrassed,

"Pat, the Lord tells me that you have a serious condition in your left breast. Now, I'm going to pray for you." I will never forget how she prayed with such sincerity and fervency. Then she turned to me and said with confidence, "Pat, the Lord tells me that He has healed you and that the pain will leave in about three days."

The next day I took Loretta and Laete to lunch. It was then that Loretta said to me, "Pat, I want to be sure that the Lord wanted me to tell you. Last night when I prayed for you, the Lord told me that you had a cancer in your left breast." That was no surprise to me because I had suspected that might be the case considering the type of pain I had experienced. As the Lord told Loretta, the pain was gone in three days, and it has never returned.

I will praise the Lord Jesus forever for being my Savior and healing me; and I will always, for eternity, have a special love for Loretta because she was willing to obey the Lord and become a vessel to be used for His glory in praying for those who are sick.

Patricia Blake

West Hollywood, CA

CANCER OF THE THYROID INSTANTLY HEALED

I was in a Ft.Worth, Texas Hospital and was diagnosed with cancer of the thyroid. The doctors said I need radiation treatment and gave me a bad report.

Loretta Blasingame came to my bedside to visit me and ask me what was wrong. I told her about my condition. She told me that her work for the Lord was to travel worldwide, conducting Healing Crusades. When I heard this, I asked her to pray and told her I wanted to live because I have two small children.

Loretta laid hands on me and prayed that God would perform a miracle. Immediately, I felt heat go through my body and I stayed in the hospital a few days more. The doctors tested me again and could not find any cancer. I have not taken any medication or radiation since that day. I am totally healed and have been for two years (since 1996).

I give Loretta Blasingame permission to use this testimony for the glory of God.

The Wi-Ro Hong family of Plano, Texas.

Sam-Rhe (wife),was healed of thyroid cancer in a Ft. Worth hospital.

Is Anybody Up There?

LEIDA CADIZ – TV STAR

Healed of Throat Nodules

We met on March 17, 1994 at **KMPX TV 29** in Dallas, TX. At the time, I was working for TV 29 as a volunteer in Accounting during the day and as needed on the prayer line at night.

You were interviewed that evening by Joni and Marcus Lamb. I had left the station and was watching the program in my bedroom. When you shared your testimony, I said a simple prayer and asked JESUS to heal me from the 2 nodules in my throat. One was visible on my neck; it's size and shape was similar to a strawberry.

Three doctors had seen me, there were lab tests done and a scan. The prescribed pills' side effects would have affected my heart. Therefore I never took a pill and I still have all 30 of them plus the medical documentation.

JESUS healed me that night as you were sharing about your healing ministry. I rushed to TV 29 to meet you and told everyone about this miracle. I am a Christian singer and it was hard for me to sing because I felt tightness in my throat.

That Friday night Joni and Marcus shared my testimony just before the program was suppose to end at 9:00 PM. Then the program was extended for another 30 minutes. At the end, you prayed for me and in your prayer you asked GOD not to allow these nodules to ever come back.

That prayer was answered. My doctors agree, I am healed! Thank You JESUS!!!

The next day, Saturday morning, I started to sing a song with very high notes which I used to struggle with before. Since then I am able to sing freely, I sing all the notes without any problems, and I had not even warmed up yet.

Today, I am serving as Sr. Pastor of a small bilingual (Spanish/ English) church, namely **ADONAI CENTRO CRISTIANO** here in Clearwater, Florida. In addition, I produce a bilingual TV program for Community Access which airs twice a week and have shared my testimony at **CHRISTIAN TELEVISION NETWORK** which reaches areas in 7 states in the southeast. There had been many more blessings!

Leida Cadiz

Clearwater, FL

“CLUSTER” HEADACHES SCATTER

I have been plagued with excruciating headaches since I was a teenager and have had surgery on two different occasions. Over the years, the headaches continued, and I had a series of histamine desensitization shots for more than a year to no avail. The headaches were diagnosed as “cluster headaches” which are considered the most powerful. All kinds of medications were prescribed, including oxygen. There were times I would awaken in severe pain five days out of seven.

When Loretta Blasingame came to our city, I was praying with a group of believers in preparation for her meeting. The Lord showed me a vision in which He said this meeting would be as the “Pool of Bethesda.” He said He was sending His servant Loretta to stir up the waters, but it would not be healing only for the first person who stepped into the water. “Whosoever” would come would be healed.

This vision proved to be true. At the Sunday evening service where she was ministering under the anointing of the Holy Spirit, Loretta said, “Someone’s brain is being healed. The Lord is restoring blood vessels, nerves, and recreating tissue, and right now that person feels like ice water is running through their head.”

As I was sitting in the congregation, it was as though she had read my neurologist’s report, and I felt as if my head was totally wrapped in “ice-hot” Mentholatum. I claimed my healing and testified with great joy. Loretta said the Lord had shown her that the healing would continue for several days, and indeed it did! What a blessed relief to wake up pain free after so many years. I am grateful each day for my healing that was purchased at Calvary and for the Lord’s precious, obedient handmaiden, Loretta.

I release this testimony for publication to the Glory of God.

Elaine Davis
North Carolina

Is Anybody Up There?

"WITHOUT MY MIRACLE OF HEALING, I WOULD HAVE BEEN HEARING IMPAIRED THE REST OF MY LIFE"

I am a physician and I work with sick people everyday. Therefore I am exposed to their ailments.

During this winter, the amount of patients I cared for had colds, sore throats and ear infections. Being exposed to sick children and adults, I contacted a severe ear infection that regardless of the first-class antibiotics I took, ruptured my tympanic membrane reducing my audition to 50% of the original level. I could barely hear from that ear. I had to wear my stethoscope on my right ear only and tell my patients that I had an infection on the other ear. It was depressing to me not being able to care for my patients properly.

The medical solution to the problem was to wait for the body to grow the rest of the membrane which was not 100% sure, or have surgery to replace the ruptured membrane with an artificial one. This remedy did not guarantee complete restoration of the hearing.

I called Evangelist Loretta Blasingame on February 23, 2006 for prayer and after she prayed for me, I noticed 50% improvement on that ear. The next day, I was able to hear 100% off my semi-deaf ear.

I thank my God for this miracle, without it, I would be a handicapped doctor for life. I also thank Loretta for her prayer and healing ministry that the Lord gave to her.

PRAISE THE LORD FOR HE IS WORTHY TO BE ADORED AND PRAISED FOREVER AND EVER.

Dr. Nilza Reich, D.O.

Bay Shore, NY

Is Anybody Up There?

"I SAID TO MYSELF: I KNOW GOD CAN HEAL...BUT HE DOESN'T NEED TO WASTE HIS TIME ON ME...BUT HE DID"

I was having a bad problem for a very long time. I was dizzy all the time--I thought everybody was dizzy all the time.

What happened to me is that I have been pregnant twice. I was really bad. I was dizzy a lot of the time. I would wake up in the middle of the night really, really sick. It was horrible. My doctor kept saying "we've done every test we know of. We don't know what's wrong."

My doctor just couldn't find anything wrong with me. So, I said "okay-- and I guess I'm just going to be dizzy and sick for the rest of my life."

So, then after I had the baby, I thought maybe my dizziness and sickness would go away, but it didn't.

In April, I went to another doctor. He found that I had this huge hole in my ear. So, he fixed it by operating on it. After three weeks, I went back because I was still dizzy. He said "well, I fixed this hole, so you are going to have to take medicine the rest of your life." What happened is I have too much fluid in my ear. So, this hole can't heal like it is supposed to.

So, while I was in the hospital, a man from my church came to visit me. He was so nice. Our church is large so, I didn't know who "Mr. Hospital Greeter" was. So, after I was released from the hospital, I eventually went back to my church.

It was Wednesday night, I found the man who came to visit me in the hospital there. So, I said "Thank God, I found Mr. Hospital Greeter." It just happened to be that an Evangelist, Loretta

Blasingame was there conducting a healing service. I was nursing my baby, and I wanted to continue doing so, but this medication the doctor put me on would cause me not to be able to nurse. It was a really difficult thing. The man at my church asked me to have Loretta pray over me. I said to him "She won't be able to do anything, please."

So the man said "can't you just have a little bit of faith, just a little bit of faith?"—I thought, I know God can heal me, but I thought God doesn't need to waste his time on me. Then the man said, "Oh no, come on over here to Loretta." So I went over there and Loretta laid her hands on me. I felt this power of God and my ears got really hot. And, her hand was all red.

So, I went home and I said to myself "I know God has healed me—I know it." I didn't tell my husband for three days, but, he knew something was wrong when I didn't have to get up sick in the middle of the night. So, by Friday, I told him what had happened at Loretta's meeting.

But, you know what? God has healed me—I don't have to take the medicine anymore. And, I can hear. My hearing is just incredible. And, the doctor said, within three weeks I would have been completely deaf.

Anyway, it's really great, and God has done a major miracle in my life. And even in the last couple of weeks. So, God is a healer.

Before God healed me, I couldn't raise my head back or down to read my piano music, so I stopped playing the piano.

The doctor said to me when he checked my ear after my healing, "It looks as though he never did an operation on your ear—there are no scars in your ear." The doctor says, "I am healed."

I am so grateful for Loretta Blasingame and her healing miracle ministry because I need my hearing. And, I need to be able to turn my neck because I am a concert pianist at Southern Methodist University here in Dallas, TX. Now, I can play and teach again. I am so grateful for my miracle. I have played the piano in Loretta's meetings to honor God for my healing.

Joan Wilson Greene, concert pianist and Southern Methodist University music instructor, gives her testimony about how the hearing in her left ear was healed. Doctors gave her only two weeks before she would have lost all hearing in that ear.

HEALED!!!!

MIRACLE "FLOATING EYE" CONDITION

WHEN PASTOR LORETTA PRAYED OVER THE PHONE

For the past year and a half, the sight in my right eye has been hindered with "floaters" which are drops of blood that block your vision. After my retina specialist performed laser treatments in his office, they still did not go away. Eventually, the doctor said I needed to go to the hospital for surgery. Privately, he was concerned that possibly he would discover a retinal tear or detachment.

I phoned Sister Loretta Blasingame in Dallas, Texas, and told her about my condition. She prayed with me over the phone, and we asked God to heal and help me.

Praise the Lord for His beautiful answers. The surgery revealed no tear or detachment of the retina, my eyesight improved promptly and nicely. I was able to return to my office job in just two weeks instead of the usual four to six weeks.

To top it all off, I experienced the peace of God in a special sense both at the time of surgery, and when I returned to work. The favor of God was not only evident in my life, but His Grace was also obviously at work in the lives of my supervisor and my fellow workers.

Gloria Whitney

Vista, CA

Arthritis Nearly Cost Me My Job…
until Jesus healed me

I attended the dinner meeting of the Durham, NC Business Men's Fellowship USA with the president, Alex Jones. I had been having chest pain, anxiety, not sleeping, developing spots on my feet, and my complexion had turned dark. In addition, my right thumb had been sore and swollen for a number of weeks. I had been making drapery for Alex for over 40 years, and at that point I almost could not cut fabric of any sort. I was deeply concerned about my situation and had made an appointment with my doctor for the following day.

Loretta Blasingame was the speaker for the evening, and during her ministry under the anointing of the Holy Spirit, she called out healing for someone with arthritis, and I felt "something," leave my right thumb. Suddenly the pain left, and the swelling was gone. I was very excited and stood to testify to my healing. The next day, I was working on heavy drapery and could cut the fabric with no problem, and still have that total healing of my thumb, for which I give God the glory.

Later in the meeting, Loretta said that someone's heart was being healed. I knew that was for me, too, and stood to claim my healing. The doctor's examination the next day gave me a clean bill of health. I've had no further chest pain and am sleeping well. The spots on my feet disappeared, and my complexion has returned to its normal condition. I thank God for his healing power through the Holy Spirit and for his obedient servant, Loretta Blasingame.

I release this testimony for publication for the Glory of God.

Mrs. Loucile Murray
Durham, NC

WHEN FRIENDS PRAY… MIRACLES HAPPEN!

Dear Loretta,

You don't know me at all, but my friend from work, Geri Hetterich, invited me a few weeks ago to your prayer service at Embassy Suites on a Friday night. I think she had seen you at her church. Here is the follow-up praise report I emailed to everyone in Geri's and my prayer group that meets every Thursday at work.

As many of you know, we've been praying for my girlfriend, Judy, who has had severe pain in her knees and ankles. She's also had gastrointestinal problems and an eating disorder.

A few weeks ago after choir rehearsal, we laid hands on her and she immediately felt a cessation of pain that allowed her to have the first uninterrupted night's sleep in two months. The pain returned and she realized the necessity of it because it motivated her to finally go to the doctor. She discussed the inevitable surgery with him.

Friday night Geri and I went to a prayer meeting led by a woman named Loretta Blasingame from Geri's church. I was 2 hours late due to working late so by the time I got there it was nearly over. I specifically had my friend Judy in mind and wanted to stand in intercessory prayer for her. Loretta had several prayer teams around the room and they would bring the person forward and the whole room would pray for the person, with Loretta leading.

Loretta made a last call for healing and said "I never usually do this, but I have a feeling from the Holy Spirit that there's someone that has been planning on surgery and we need to pray for this person." No one went forward to claim the healing, so I figured the Lord had to be meaning Judy. Geri and I went up to Loretta, and with the help of several of her prayer team members, we prayed for Judy to receive the love being offered from Our Lord via His Holy Spirit.

I could hardly wait until Sunday morning when I'd see Judy again; it was very tempting not to call her ahead of time, but on Sunday there she was, bopping around the church just like the old days. "Gee Jude," I queried, "You look mighty perky."

Judy went on to tell me that she saw her doctor (finally!) Tuesday but was despondent because the medication he put her on didn't make any difference by Friday. But when she woke up Saturday morning, she felt FABULOUS! She still needs to continue the regimen the Doc has prescribed for her, but now the surgery is "optional" instead of mandatory. God is good, AMEN!"

In the warmth of Jesus' heart.

Jan Bordeleau

THERE IS NO DISTANCE IN PRAYER

WHEN YOU PRAYED FOR ME ON THE PHONE I WAS HEALED—

I would like to thank you for being such a faithful servant and always standing in the gap for His people. Throughout the years that I have known you, I have watched you pray for countless people and give inexhaustibly to meet every need. Through your prayers on the phone to me in Big Bear Lake, California as we were visiting, you spoke a word of knowledge over me and said, "Father, my sister is on the verge of being a diabetic."

I remember how dynamically you prayed for me, taking dominion and speaking out the provision God has given us in Christ. And while you were praying, I felt a tingle go through my body, and I knew God touched me. I didn't know exactly what He did then, but later on during the day, I noticed the craving for sweets that I had were suddenly gone, and to this day that overpowering craving urge has never returned.

You also prayed for a number of other things at that time, including a release on the selling of our house that we so desperately wanted to sell for two years. We sold that home shortly after in 2 days with the buyers putting $87,000 down. I stand in awe when I think of our Lord who is on our side and mightily in battle, leading us into VICTORY!

Your friend and sister in Christ,

Sandra Witt

Big Bear, CA

Is Anybody Up There?

A MIRACLE REUNION OF SON WITH HIS BIOLOGICAL PARENTS

Dear Loretta:

I am writing to you to let you know that the word you gave my husband came to pass. He was adopted out at age three. He also has a biological brother and sister whom he found when he was seventeen. We searched for his biological mother and father, but we couldn't find them. We had very little to go on.

When you came to our church (New Beginnings) on May 24th, 1997, you told him that in the very near future he would find his biological parents. Not quite three months later, on a quiet evening, the phone rang and it was his biological brother. He told him that their mother had been in touch with his adopted mother.

A week later, we cried tears of joy as we got to speak to both my husband's biological mother and father. Later, they came and spent two weeks shortly before Christmas at our home. I can't begin to tell you what a blessing it is to know these two wonderful people. My husband got answers to a lot of questions.

Our newly found parents and grandparents really love our children. They are real grandparents. They read stories and played games with them almost constantly until they had to go back home to New York. It was a special Christmas for us all. We thank God for this glorious miracle.

We appreciate your prophetic word and your prayers. We hope you will be in our area again soon.

Enclosed, please find a check to help you in your work. We pray that God will continue to bless you.

Melissa Davies
Burnsville, Minnesota

FROM ATTEMPTED SUICIDE TO THE PULPIT!

I would just like to say thank God for his precious gift of Jesus Christ and the Holy Ghost. With both of them, you can do anything.

As a little child growing up, I never felt that I fit in. I grew older, and I would try and try to make things right-- but it just never seemed to work. So, I would just run from things and hide things until finally I made a promise to myself that I would never be run over again by people, or let anyone intimidate me. I became what you might say a "rascal". I was hard to live with when things didn't go my way.

I began to drink to fit in with my uncles and other people he ran with. At nine years old, I would drink a case of beer a day just to try to fit in.

As time went on I drank more and more, I would turn to sex or whatever to fill the void—stealing, fighting, staying out—just never being fulfilled. I got into racing cars, whatever, just to fill that void. I began to hang out with the wrong crowd and did only what I wanted to do. I would get drunk and abuse my daughter. Afterwards, when I sobered up, I would just stand in front of the mirror and cry out to God because I knew I was a sinner and all this was wrong.

My mother told me about God. It was not my mother's fault that I turned out the way I did.

Needless to say, I continued to run from God. I knew God had a calling on my life. I knew God was real, because I would make promises to Him that if He would do this that or another, I would do "this that or another". And, God would always come through.

In March of 1990, me, my son, and my nephew were in the truck going to buy some more beer. I had warrants out for my arrest.

We had already talked to the District Attorney about making a deal for some things that I had done. In due time the sheriff sent two carloads of officers out to arrest me. Eventually I was arrested and sentenced to 99 years. Finally, because of my mother's prayers and God's mercy, I got out on a personal bond.

Instead of thanking God and all the others who had helped me, I said to my wife, "This is it—I'm going to get me some beer and I going to get drunk and I'm going to commit suicide."

I went by to see my mother and brother and I told them what I was going to do. I was like, you know, I can't face going to prison for 99 years! Somehow, I was going to get to the river and end it all.

The river was raging and had full banks. I had made up my mind that I would just shoot myself and fall in the river and then I would be out of my troubles.

I didn't have enough sense to know that this would just be the beginning of my troubles. Yet I attempted to take my life twice. Each time I stopped. I was still drinking and calling out to God. I had tried so many other things, but still knew that God was the only way. The third time I attempted to do it, but stopped again.

I had cocked my pistol and I said, "Okay Lord this is it, if you don't tell me what to do I'm just going to pull the trigger". And, God spoke to my heart and said "Put that stuff down."

He said, "You go to the house and you get cleaned up and go to church."

So, I went home, cleaned up and told my mother that "I was going to make Jesus Lord of my life." I told her that I didn't want anybody going with me, I just wanted to go see the pastor that was hosting the revival by myself. I went and talked with the Pastor and he said the sinner's prayer with me.

God had sent a special lady, Evangelist [Loretta Blasingame], to this particular church to conduct a revival. It was only supposed to run a short while, but it turned out to be 5 weeks!

Every night I would go and cry out to God. I was hurting so bad inside. I wasn't worried about going to prison anymore because I knew that God would take care of it. That was how much faith I had put in God.

I began to trust the Lord more and more. I remember the night that the evangelist, "Sister Loretta" prayed for me. The devil came out of me.

Some people ask, "Well how can that be when you've been saved?" I won't go into any details, but, I know what happened, and I was baptized in the Holy Ghost. And, I have thanked God for that day every since.

I just want to say thank the Lord because He was there and never left me. I have since learned that I have to be continually hooked up to Jesus. So many times we fall into a world that is so busy and demanding all of our time from God. But, God says "...seek Him first and His righteousness and all these other things will be added unto you."

If anyone reading this happens to be doing things that are wrong even though you are in church--because I know that there are people who do it all of the time, don't run from God—run to Him. God knows everything. You cannot hide anything from God no matter what. Run to Him because He is always there with open arms. He will not turn you away. Let Him renew your heart so that you will stay close up to Him.

Don't let the devil win because he is not going to ever stop trying to deceive you until you meet God Almighty. And God said "Well done thy good and faithful servant. Enter in to the joy of rest." I pray that you will not turn your back on God, but continue to trust Him no matter how hard it gets—no matter how many temptations come. He will make a way of escape.

ADENDUM

Jimmy Driver's mother Maggie Ward, found her son with a gun to his head. He was going to kill himself over having abused his daughter, who was then 11 years old. He was facing years in prison. Maggie and Jimmy's wife Marie, talked him into coming to one of the miracle services. Loretta prayed for him and he was delivered from alcoholism. He received the baptism of the Holy Spirit. Loretta testified at his trial for sexual assault.

Jimmy was sentenced to 10 years probation and $10,000 fine. God has completely healed their family and reunited them. Their daughter was taken away from them at the age of 12 and was returned just prior to her 16th birthday. Forgiveness, repentance and reconciliation has brought Jimmy and his family back together.

Jimmy is now serving the Lord as the Volunteer Chaplain at the Ferguson Unit at the Texas Department of Criminal Justice. His daughter now married, has blessed him and his wife with a beautiful granddaughter.

Jimmy N. & Marie Driver

Madisonville, TX

Families Healed

Kevin and Kristy Merritt were unable to conceive a second child until Loretta Blasingame prayed for her. One year later, Loretta returned to dedicate their daughter to God. Kristy's sister had a similar experience at the same time.

Angelica Hernandez holds her baby, Guadalupe, who was healed when she received two new eyes (she had been blind), was given a new heart and a new brain. Here they appear on TBN in Phoenix, with Loretta Blasingame, who prayed for the baby in the hospital.
The doctors had planned to take the baby off life support.

PART THREE

My Favorite Sermons and Devotions

Is Anybody Up There?

THE ABRAHAMIC COVENANT

Abraham was in his own country when God spoke to him and said:

"Get thee out of thy country, and from thy kindred and from thy father's house, unto a land that I will show thee" (Genesis 12:6).

Do you wonder, like many of God's people wonder, why you are not being blessed? Could it be because you don't know what His promises are to you?

The answer is, God has promised us His substance, but we have to know what God has promised us in order to receive it. We know God has established a bank account for us in heaven, and when we are in need of something, we can just come to the Father and write a check on our bank account. How does that happen? Let's look at the life of Abraham.

It is interesting that God would speak to Abraham and say, "I want you to get up. I want you to leave this country. I want you to even leave your kindred, as I am going to take you to a land that you don't know anything about. But, I will reveal it to you when I get you there."

I can imagine what Abraham was thinking at this point, "God, I'm glad I have my full trust and faith in you. So I can trust you for where your are going to take me, and that you are going to take care of me."

Some of you may be in a place where God has brought you, and you may be saying, "God, have you forgotten me?"

No. God has not forgotten you. He knows exactly where you are, every day, every hour. Not one child of God is in a place not known by our Father.

And further, God says to Abraham: *I will make of thee a great nation; and I will bless thee, and make thy name great..." (Genesis 12:2).*

Today, you and I are the seed of Abraham, and to those who bless the seed of Abraham, God will give a special blessing. He will bless those that bless Abraham and his seed. This means every child of God is now under the covenant that God gave to Abraham. You are blessed.

From the very beginning, God had the whole plan already mapped out, even before Abraham was born. Likewise, today, God has the plan and purpose for your life already mapped out. In heaven, the Holy Trinity—God, Jesus, and the Holy Spirit—sat down and decided the direction for our lives even before we were born.

At times we find ourselves fretting, living in fear, wondering whether God knows what He is doing, or perhaps we wonder what God is doing on our behalf. Be encouraged today. God knows exactly what He is doing in your life, and this is where faith comes in.

Notice that Abraham had the blessings of God, and the Covenants of God. According to Genesis:

Abraham went up out of Egypt, he and his wife and all that he had, and Lot with him into the south, and Abram was very rich, in cattle, in silver, and in gold (Genesis 13:1-2).

Some might have a problem that God's children should be wealthy. It is an established fact that God gave the same promise to you and me that He gave to Abraham. In the book of Romans, Paul verifies our inclusion in the Covenant of Abraham in the New Testament (Romans 4).

He made Abraham very wealthy in cattle, silver and gold because of the covenant God had given him. In that day, the people who saw Abraham, knew the blessings of God were upon him.

Then God said to Abraham, *"When you get to the land that I will show you, I want you to look; and all the land as far as you can see, I will give it to you and to your seed, forever" (paraphrase Genesis 13:14-15).*

Remember, the "forever" of Romans said, *"And He blessed him as said, blessed he Abraham of the Most High God, possessor of heaven and earth"(Genesis 14:19).*

God gave such a mighty blessing to Abraham that he was called "a possessor of heaven" because of the most High God. It was a Sovereign gift. Therefore, under the Covenant of God to Abraham, you and I can also be a "possessor of heaven and earth."

Do you know why all that God has belongs to you and me? It is because we have been adopted into the family of God. We belong to the Most High God. That is a tremendous covenant, which we must never forget.

When in fear, when in anger, when in strife, when in lack, and when you don't know what to do, or you are in the midst of the storm, you need to just simply stop, and for one moment, remember to Whom you belong. You belong to the Most High God who is the possessor of heaven and earth, and He has adopted you into His family.

Oftentimes, people say to me, "Pray for me, Loretta. I don't have any family."

I always reply, "You have been adopted into the family of God. You have a very large family, because God has children all over this world."

All, who are led by the Spirit of God, are the sons of God. So you have a big family. Don't ever feel like you are in this world alone.

First, you are never alone. You belong to The Most High God. Second, God has not forgotten where you are, and He has not forgotten who you are, nor has He forgotten your name.

God gave another great promise to Abraham:

And when Abram was ninety years old and nine, the LORD appeared to Abram, and said unto him, I am the Almighty God; walk before me, and be thou perfect (Genesis 17:1).

He is going to bless him. Never say never —Abram was then 99 years old.

Today, we are under this covenant. It would be a good thing to remind the Lord, and yourself, each day, "I am under the Covenant of Abraham. You have promised me that you will multiply me exceedingly. You have promised me that you will keep your covenant with me."

Do you believe God talks to us today? Sometimes people say to me, "God doesn't talk to us today." I know they say it in ignorance. They really don't mean it, because if they knew the *Bible*, they couldn't make this statement. Abram fell on his face and God talked with him

Wouldn't it be sad if our God, who created this universe, was not able to talk to us? The Lord speaks to me everyday. Sometimes, I'm so busy I don't hear His voice, but He says, "My sheep know my voice." Why would the Lord say that unless he speaks to us?

As God continued to speak to Abraham, He said: "*As for me, behold, my covenant is with thee, and thee shalt be a father of many nations" (Genesis 17:4).*

And then God said, *"Is any thing too hard for the*

Lord ?"(Genesis 18:14).

And the answer is, of course not. Abraham was promised a son when he and Sarah were past the age of child bearing. But God promised, and in due season, the child was born.

Then, to prove his faith, God tempted him by telling him he must offer Isaac. God was still walking so close to Abraham that his faith was still rising.

The story is told in Chapter 22 of Genesis. In obedience to God, we find Abraham on the mountain with Isaac. And Abraham speaks to the servant who came with them: "*Abide ye here with the ass. I and the lad will go yonder and worship and will come again to you" (Genesis 22:3).*

Abraham said, *''We will go and worship God."*

He didn't say, "I'm going to go up to the mountain, and kill my son; you better call people to pray for me, because I will soon be in a grieving state."

He said, *"I and the lad will go worship God."*

Abraham had great faith in God. He knew God would make provision. (You may read this whole account in Genesis, Chapter 22).

This great blessing and covenant God gave Abraham is reiterated in Genesis 22:17, *"I will bless thee and multiply thy seed as the stars of the heaven. And as the sand on the sea shore; and thy seed shall possess the gate of his enemy."*

God told Abraham over and over He would bless him and multiply him. God is not in the subtracting business. He is in the multiplying business. And sometimes, God repeats a promise over and over because, we, as human beings, tend to forget.

To emphasize His promise even more, *God said, "Look up at the stars at night and you can see the blessings of God, that will instill this covenant, and during the daytime, you can go by the sea shore and see the sand and know this is still YOUR COVENANT" (paraphrased Genesis 33:17).*

In this covenant it says further, *"Thy seed shall possess the gate of his enemy."* God added a clause here to say, we will "possess the gate of our enemy." You don't have to worry about your enemies. God promised in this covenant He will take care of our enemies. Know this hour, you can sit down and write a check on the bank you have in heaven, because this is the Covenant of God to you and me. Claim it!

I CAN DO ALL THINGS THROUGH CHRIST

The Apostle Paul said: *"I can do all things through Christ, who strengtheneth me" (Philippians 4:13).*

Paul knew the strength of God. He knew that within himself he could do nothing. He also said, "*of all the sinners I'm the chief*..." *(1 Timothy 1:15).* Yet, he knew the power of God.

The Apostle Paul experienced great tribulations and sufferings. He was a man who truly knew what suffering for Christ meant. He emphatically declared, *"I was hungry. I was cold. I was fasting and yet I glory in my infirmities" (paraphrased 2 Corinthians 11th Chapter).* That had to have come from a man who had an encounter with God, who had fellowship with God, and had been strengthened in his trials.

In 2 Cor.13:14, Paul was speaking about the love of God, and communion with Him. The verse states, *"The grace of the Lord Jesus Christ and the love of God, and the communion of the Holy Ghost be with you all!"*

There is an important key in that Scripture regarding the communion of the Holy Ghost. We, as Christians, are to have communion with the Holy Ghost as Paul did. That is why he could say:

> *"I was in weariness, I was in painfulness, I was in watching, often in hunger, thirst, and fasting, coldness and nakedness. Beside those things that are without that which cometh upon me daily, the cares of all the churches" (paraphrased 2 Corinthians 11:1).*

When he asked the Lord about the thorn in his flesh, the Lord answered and said, "...*My grace is sufficient for thee" (2 Corinthians 12:9).*

That was good enough for Paul who said:

"Therefore, I take pleasure in infirmities, in reproaches, in necessities, in persecutions, in distresses for Christ sake; For when I am weak then I am strong" (2 Corinthians 12:10).

So Paul was a man who knew the strengths of God. That is why he could say: *"I can do all things through Christ who strengtheneth me" (Philippians 4:13).*

With Christ, we can do all things. There are times we go through trials and tribulations, and we don't know what to do. We don't know which way to turn. It seems like there is no way our situation can turn around. You may be thinking you are in the midst of a trial, which maybe God himself cannot turn around, but I can encourage you today; you can do all things through Christ who strengthens you. You CAN make it through the day with Christ.

The Word of God says, *"Thy shoes shall be iron and brass; and as thy days, so shall thy strength be" (Deuteronomy 33:25).*

Do you know God zeroes in on THIS day? He wants you to know this particular day is so important, that He will come to you today in the midst of your trial in mercy and grace, and power through His Holy Spirit.

Jesus has promised us enough of His love for one day at a time, enough of His strength for one day at a time. By His enabling grace He sustains us. You can look to Jesus and know God in heaven has placed within you the Lord Jesus Christ, to help you make this day.

The Lord carried me in the midst of the greatest trial of my life. I lost my only son, Rickey, who was only 24 years of age at the time. He had always served the Lord, and loved God. I was devastated when he died, but the Lord helped me.

In times like this, all His virtues are manifestly expressed in His counsel, by His love, in His mercy, in His healing, in His grace, in His provision, and with His strength.

There is no pain like the death of a loved one, especially your child. But by the Comforter, the Holy Spirit, we can rise again, put our grief on the back that bore our sorrows at Calvary, and by the promise that Lord Jesus will never leave us nor forsake us.

With Jesus' help, I now know I can do all things through Christ. He helped me each day to know I could do all things through Christ. YOU can do all things through Christ. Lean on Him this very hour.

Place your hand in the hand of God. Trust Him, and you can do all through Christ. Let God have communion with you today. Let Him have time with you starting today. When His Holy Spirit lives within you, you can do all things.

"I KNOW THE WAY THAT YOU TAKE...."

"He knows the way that I take" (Job 23:10).

Soon after my only son, Rickey, died, I experienced one of the worst nights I'd had since his death. I was praying and crying as I held Rickey's guitar close; I prayed all night, and in God's compassion, He gave me a direct word, speaking to me once again to let me know He knew where I was and He came to comfort me. His words were, "I know the way that you take."

After hearing His voice, the Holy Spirit impressed me to open the Bible. It opened to **Job 23:10,** and I read Job's words, the same words God had just spoken to me:

"He knows the way that I take."

As I meditated on these words, I saw that Job is testifying in the midst of a great storm in his life. He had lost all his property and all his ten children, and yet, in the midst of the storm he cried out in solid faith, *"He knoweth the way that I take; when He has tried me, I shall come forth as gold" (Job 22:10).*

In spite of the storm's buffeting, he was stating that God knows our storms, and He knows about the trials in our lives, but He will be by our side to help and sustain us. Jesus, the incredible Creator of the universe, the One who carries the governments upon His shoulders, promises in the scriptures, *"I will never leave thee nor forsake thee" (Hebrews 13:5).*

I would like to direct you to another path, the one that Jesus, the Lamb of God, took. God knew the path His Son would take. As John said, *"Behold the Lamb of God" (John 1:29).*

He was the Lamb that came to be slain for you and me. Today, we can look to the cross for victory because of the Lamb that was slain. Because His sin-cleansing, devil-defeating blood was shed on the cross, and in turn, Jesus said we are to take up our cross daily, and follow Him.

I'm reminded of an old hymn that says:

Alas, and did my Savior bleed,
and did my Savior die.
Would He devote that sacred head for
such a worm as I.
At the cross, at the cross
where I first saw the light,
and my burdens rolled away.
It was there by faith
I received my sight,
and now I am happy all the day.

Because of the Cross, you and I can have every confidence that our Savior can carry us through the storms and trials and direct our paths.

Job said, "*He knoweth the way that I take and when He hath tried me I shall come forth as gold.*"

Job further says, *"I know my redeemer liveth" (Job 19:25).*

Job knew one thing, he did not understand his trials and all he had lost, but because he knew God and he could look up in the face of it all and say, "*I know my redeemer liveth. My ears have heard His words, but now my eyes seeth Him" (paraphrase Job 13:1).*

I want you to know you do not have to fear when the darkened clouds are gathered about you. The God we serve cares and understands. The storms we face threaten us and they confound us, but of this I am assured, my hand is in His, and you can place your hands in His today, and you, too, can say I'm in His capable hands. Whatever the future holds, I am in His hands.

The days that I cannot see have all been planned (by God) for me. His way is best because I am in His hands. Although I cannot know the way that lies before me, I still can trust and freely follow His commands. My faith is firm, because it is He that watches over me. Of this I am confident, I am in His hands.

When the hands of Jesus were stretched out on the cross on Calvary's hill, He paid the price that you may say as Job said, "*I know that my Redeemer liveth";* and I know the path that I take because I know the Redeemer.

We may not know and understand the storms, but we do know one thing, and in this one thing we are confident, our hands have been placed in the hands of Jesus, and because of His nail-scarred hands, He can carry us in the midst of every storm.

You may feel you have lost everything. You may feel life is over. You may feel you do not have a reason to live. I say to you, because of Calvary and what it stands for, because of the shed blood of Jesus, that wonderful miracle-working power of the blood of Jesus can still work for you. We have power through His divine blood. Be confident and know because of the Lamb slain for you, that precious blood still has power.

Oh! How I praise the Lamb that was slain at Calvary to pay the price for every trial we will ever go through.

I want you to know every trial has been paid for. I want you to know that Jesus knows every heartache. He knows every grief you bare. He not only knows the heartaches, the trials and grief, He knows the path you take and he carries you every step of the way.

"Jesus is close to those whose hearts are breaking..." (Psalms 34:18).

As you travel that rugged path, He places His hand in yours to take you through. I point you to Calvary for whatever you need, God is going to answer your prayers. Look to Calvary and close your eyes. Imagine those beautiful hands, feet and arms of Jesus stretched out on the cross.

And, always remember, Job looked toward the Cross in his storms and trials, and now, you can look back to the Cross and say, The price was paid for all my storms and trials at Calvary. He knows the way that I take and when He has tried me I shall come forth as gold!

PRAYER

Father, in the wonderful name of Jesus, I am confident that you know the path that I take. I ask, not only for myself, but for everyone in the midst of a storm, whether it be the loss of a love one, or the loss of a job, finances, despair, or not knowing where to go, what to say or what to do; I point them to Calvary. I point them to the nail scarred hands that say to us, in this one thing you can be confident, the Lamb of God was slain to redeem you for all sin and death that you may triumph. He knows the way that you take. Amen.

HOW TO HANDLE GRIEF AND SORROW AFTER THE DEATH OF A LOVED ONE

Grief and sorrow are two of the strongest emotions mankind can suffer. On the opposite scale the most profound emotional experience is love. The love of Jesus Christ is the worthiest of treasures. It is this gift of love that, in His immeasurable compassion, meets you in your anguish, and sustains you in his sweet mercy. No hurt or shame is too great for God's merciful love.

God suffered all we suffer. God grieved more than we can imagine as He watched His only Son die. God the Son felt emotionally and physically—grief, pain and death. The *Bible* says we shall have trials and suffering. At some time in our lives, we will suffer the painful loss of a loved one.

On February 19, 1991, after returning home from lunch, I received a message that my only child, Rickey Lee Blasingame, a precious young man who served the Lord with all his heart, had been shot to death in his car in a little town outside of Dallas, Texas. He was only 24 years old. My first response was disbelief. But, as I faced the pain of loss, I suffered such devastation and grief that I can only describe it as a living death.

Only a few weeks before this happened, Rickey came to my office and we had a precious time of prayer. And now, I am told he was found shot to death. March 18, just a month later, I received another dreadful phone call; my aunt had died of a heart attack. Then, on March 25, 1991, I received a phone call that my older brother had died of a heart attack. Not even a month later, June 3, 1991, the phone rang to deliver another message of death. I was told to come to the hospital. One of my older brothers passed away that morning.

From February 19th to June 3rd, I lost my only child, my aunt, and two brothers.

This was not the first time that I and my family had to deal with the shock and grief of untimely deaths. On the afternoon of Christmas Day in 1968, my dear brother-in-law, J.B. Askew, died December, 25, 1968 of a heart attack at home before the paramedics could arrive. Then on July 8, 1978, my oldest sister, Doris Askew, died after only a few months of being diagnosed with breast cancer and colon cancer. Their only child, my nephew, J. D. Askew, was left alone without either parent. Each of these deaths were agonizing times for the entire family.

Your emotions go through stages, which you may not recognize as part of the grief and healing process. It is vital you know how to allow God to help you in these very difficult times in your life.

In the Scripture, Isaiah states God can reveal his arm to you. You will need to know how to hold on to the arm of God during this agonizing period.

Isaiah is speaking of the Lord when he writes: *"Who has believed our report? And to whom is the arm of the revealed" (Isaiah 53:1)?* Verses 2 through 5 tell us Jesus is acquainted with grief and sorrow; so He is able to understand our sufferings today.

> *For He shall grow up before him as a tender plant, and as a root out of a dry ground; he hath no form not comeliness; and when we shall see him, there is no beauty that we should desire him. He is despised and rejected of men; a man of sorrows, and acquainted with grief; and we hid as it were our faces from him; he was despised, and we esteemed him not. Surely he hath borne our griefs, and carried our sorrows; yet we did esteem him stricken, smitten of God, and afflicted. But he was wounded for our transgressions, he was bruised for our iniquities; the chastisement of our peace was upon him; and with his stripes we are healed (Isaiah 53:1-5).*

How To Deal With Grief and Sorrow After Death

We will certainly have grief in our life from time to time; and we will have sorrow. The question is what do we do when great sorrow comes? What do we do when grief is so heavy it seems our heart has stopped, and when we are paralyzed with grief? Even the words of others when spoken to us, seem as if we never heard them.

After the death of a loved one, you need to be with a loving friend. You need to allow someone to be your personal friend, who like God, can reach out his arm for you to lean on. You need a natural arm, someone in the natural to whom you can relate. They will help make your walk through these times a sustaining force.

I want to help you recognize the different emotional stages you go through after a death.

1. **The first stage is grief.**

This can be almost paralyzing. You have no feeling. You won't be able to believe it really happened. The grief can so overwhelm you; there will be times you won't want to talk about it. Yet, you need to talk about it. The best way to heal grief is to talk about it.

2. **The second stage is anger.**

You feel angry at God first. Then you become angry with yourself. Often you turn your anger on your companion. You will feel anger toward the world because you cannot accept the fact you have lost someone you loved dearly.

Anger will overtake you and destroy you, unless you allow God to come in to reveal your true feelings, and why you are reacting this way. Ask God to take the anger away. It is a day by day process.

You will often hate yourself and turn anger toward yourself. You may feel there was something more you could have done to spare your loved one's life. You will feel wounded because people lack the words to comfort you, when the truth is, they don't know what to do for you. In not knowing what to do or to say, they sometimes pull away from you.

3. **There is a lack of peace in your heart**.

You will no longer know if it is possible to find peace. Sleepless nights plague you. This is where you will have to let the Word of God work for you. The word says, when we lay down we are to have *"sweet sleep."*

At first, it will be hard to apply the Scriptures you have read, but you must continue to say to God, I am going to lay down, and I am going to apply the Word of God to my life; and I will have sweet sleep tonight.

In the morning you may find you still have no peace. Again, you feel very hurt, grieved and wounded. Anger arises once more. You will wonder if you will ever have peace again.

Let me assure you, the Word of God says*, "He keepeth him in perfect peace whose mind is stayed on thee"(paraphrase of Isaiah 26:3).* You will have to realize your loved one, if they knew God, is with God. Say to yourself, "*God, they are with you! I release them, and I am going to keep my mind upon You."*

You must force yourself to keep your mind upon God. It is vital. As you keep your mind on God, you can begin to pour out your heart to God. You can come to God in honesty. You can come to God and tell Him you have no peace; you hurt; you are angry; you grieve. You can tell God everything and release it to Him in trust. God in turn will begin to pour in His healing oil.

As God begins to pour in the oil, say to God, " Lord, take this situation, this circumstance which is so devastating. Pour in the oil, and as you pour in the oil, help me some way, somehow, to find the good in this. Help me to turn this tragedy around and use it for your glory." At times it will be very difficult for you even to pray. When you cannot pray, and you have no peace, you simply can wait, as you are still before God.

The Word of God says, "*Be still and know that I am God"(Psalm 46:10).* When we are still before God, He will come to us. Though you sit quietly, you may not be able to pray, not even able to speak, but you can cry out to the Lord in your heart, and He will hear you and comfort you.

David said, *"I cried unto the Lord and he heard me"(Psalm 120:1).* This is a day by day process. Jesus has made provision for you. There is not one day, not one mood, not one emotion, and not one tear that rolls down your cheek that God doesn't understand. He knows how you feel.

There is no suffering which he has not already suffered or one trial he has not been through. Not one circumstance. Jesus suffered everything you and I will ever go through or experience. The *Bible* says**,** *"He took upon him all of our iniquities, all our sins, and all of our grief."* The prophet Isaiah said, *"Surely he has borne our griefs, and carried our sorrows…" and "the chastisement of our peace was upon him"(Isaiah 53:5).*

Through Jesus, we can have the peace of God. Through Jesus we can have the presence of God. Most of all through Jesus we can be healed of grief, and the Holy Spirit will comfort us.

4. **The stage of loneliness.**

You will feel lonelier than you have ever felt. The loneliness may overwhelm you. It may leave you with a feeling of not knowing what to do.

The Scripture the Lord gave me was, *"I will never leave thee nor forsake thee. I will be with thee even till the end of time" (paraphrased Hebrew 13:5).*

But, we have to allow Jesus to be with us. We have to acknowledge Him. His perfect love will heal our pain.

HEALING AND THE ATONEMENT

"Surely he hath borne our griefs, and carried our sorrows: yet we did esteem him stricken, smitten of God, and afflicted. But he was wounded for our transgressions, he was bruised for our iniquities; the chastisement of our peace was upon him; and with his stripes we are healed" (Isaiah 53:5).

Grief and sorrow come in different ways. The Word of God says, "*...surely he hath.*" Surely meaning: assurance or confidence; in a sure, unhesitating manner; without a doubt; assuredly; unquestionably; certainly; tied together; guaranteed. Have no doubt, the Atonement is a finished work.

I have experienced deep grief at the death of loved ones, particularly, my only son, Rickey. That kind of suffering is a grief we can't bear without divine help. Early on, I learned that, in the Atonement, Jesus paid the price for our griefs, carrying our griefs, and our sorrows.

I have also experienced much sorrow in my life. Sometimes it was an emotional sorrow, and other times physical impoverishment. My father was an alcoholic, and as a result, he was not in our lives much of the time, nor did we have material things like the other children. These were physical sorrows. But even as a child, Jesus saw my need and helped me through those times in my childhood.

In addition to Jesus carrying our griefs and sorrows, His death was an atonement for the souls of mankind, a spiritual healing. The blood atonement through Christ's death was for our emotional, physical and spiritual infirmities.

One of my favorite passage declares, *"But we see Jesus, who was made a little lower than the angels for the suffering of death, crowned with glory and honor; that he by the grace of God should taste death for every man" (Hebrews 2:9).*

It restates *John 3:16, "For God so loved...."*

Healing is just as much a part of the atonement as Salvation. The two equate to a total healing. Many times after Jesus has touched a person through a healing, it will cause him to believe in God. I truly believe you cannot be touched by God physically or emotionally without being touched spiritually. Sooner or later they will recognize a divine work in their life.

Many times in the middle of a miracle service, while people are being healed, the unbelievers will walk down the aisle, crying to the Lord asking for forgiveness, and repenting of their sins. They are wanting to be born again, even without my having given an altar call. It was the Holy Spirit moving on their hearts. Spiritual healing is the greatest of all healing—God's greatest miracle.

When the Holy Spirit performs miracles, He causes people to die to self-belief and to believe Jesus is real, and that He is to be served as the Lord of their lives.

"Surely, he hath borne,... surely he carried,... surely he was wounded,... and surely by his stripes we were healed"(Isaiah 53:5).

Some say healing and miracles were done away with; and that the Atonement through Jesus' death and resurrection, is not valid today. What Jesus paid for on the cross is for us, as long as we are on earth, extending into forever and ever. Isaiah the prophet proclaimed:

> *"For born unto us, a son is given: and the government shall be upon his shoulder: and his name shall be called Wonderful, Counselor, The mighty God, The everlasting Father, THE PRINCE OF PEACE" (Isaiah 9:5).*

Miracles are given to glorify God, and to draw men and women to Jesus Christ. In the Atonement, a finished work was surely done. Jesus declared it Himself, on the cross, ***"It is finished."***

GOD'S MASTERPIECE

"And God said, let us make man in our image, after our likeness; and let them have dominion over the fish of the sea, and over the fowl of the air, and over the cattle, and over all the earth, and every creeping thing that creepeth upon the earth"(Genesis 1:26).

Beloved, we worship a God of love. A God who is all-powerful. A God who created all things. A God who has all knowledge. A God who is ever present. This God created man in His own image and in His own likeness.

What is meant by "the image of God?" We are not only to look like him, but it means, *in the image and likeness,* we are to *act* like God. Our constant prayer should be that we become more like Him.

God made man perfect. God made Adam and Eve and put them in the beautiful Garden of Eden, a place that was perfection, full of bliss, love, harmony and unity. Perfect creatures in a perfect surrounding. There was no sickness, no pain, no woe, and no sin. They were truly the image of God. These wonderful people were not sons of God. They were the creations of God.

Satan entered the garden and consequently sin entered the garden. Adam and Eve failed. That was the beginning of sin and sickness to all mankind. We lost our God-like image in the spiritual realm, not in the physical realm. The mighty God, who made man, mercifully continued to provide for him in the garden and hereafter.

"For God so loved the world, that He gave His only begotten Son; that whosoever believeth in Him shall not perish; but have everlasting life" (John 3:16).

We have God, the Holy Spirit. Jesus redeemed our soul and the precious Holy Spirit is for the body. God is capable of taking care of His masterpiece, the human body.

David said in *Psalms 139:14, "I am fearfully and wonderfully made."* No man understands the wonderful makings of God's masterpiece. Scientists and doctors marvel at how wonderfully man is made. We are God's masterpiece. A masterpiece is the ultimate of one's creativity.

God allows me to see some of these wonders as I pray for peoples' healing. He shows me how easy it is for man to take the glory. God looked down upon us, and He saw right into our body's body. He can see what is causing the pain, and He knows just what to do. And He does it so willingly, so gladly. We praise the Lord for the work. God brought deliverance.

All machinery is patterned after the human body. Consider the heart. It is the engine and the pump. It is a massive muscle, weighing approximately 3/4 of a pound. It beats more than 60-80 times a minute, a hundred thousand times a day, forty million times a year. It exerts enough energy every 14 hours to raise a two-pound weight twelve miles into the air. It moves more than 10 tons of blood in 24 hours.

The heart never rests more than a fraction of a second at a time. The heart keeps on working until God says it is enough. God made the heart, in itself a marvelous creation.

The next time you sing the lovely little chorus, "come into my heart, come into my heart Lord Jesus. Come in today, come in to stay. Come into my heart, Lord Jesus," remember God made your heart and He can come in — only, you must invite Him.

Let's examine the mind. The mind is the smallest camera in the world. It not only takes pictures but also retains them and hangs them in the art gallery of our memory. Pictures of our past and the present reside in our memory, and they influence our whole life.

Sometimes these things are not good, or are unpleasant. Sometimes friends and loved ones don't understand, but beloved God understands.

"Thou hast searched me, and known me. Thou knowest my downsitting and mine uprising, thou understandest my thought afar off"(Psalms 139).

It seems that God looked down on earth before the creation of man and wanted fellowship with more than the angels. God made man and had fellowship with him. God greatly desires our fellowship. God wants our worship. God gave his only begotten Son for us.

Put your faith and trust in God today. He made you. He provides for every need you have. *"Cast not away therefore your confidence, which hath great recompence of reward" (Hebrews 10:35).*

You are God's masterpiece, fearfully and wonderfully made. Made for what purpose? You are made to be sons of God — the manifested sons of God; joint heirs with Christ! God has entrusted to you the great privilege of winning souls. You are the priest of God. You are God's intercessors. Your are coworkers together with Jesus.

Paul said, *"For me to live is Christ, and to die, is gain" (Philippians 1:21),* meaning, He lives in me, to do His will as Christ did God's will. We are fearfully and wonderfully made for His glory.

Psalms 8:3-9 expresses:

> *When I consider thy heavens, the work of thy fingers, the moon and the stars, which thou hast ordained; What is man, that thou art mindful of him? and the son of man that thou visitest him.*
>
> *For thou has made him a little lower than the angels and hast crowned him with glory and honor. Thou*

> *madest him to have dominion over the works of thy hands; thou hast put all things under his feet. All sheep and oxen, yea, and the beasts of the field; the fowl of the air, and the fish of the sea, and whatsoever passeth through the paths of the seas. O Lord our Lord, how excellent is thy name in all the earth.*

Have you ever noticed how many stars there are at night? They glisten from unbelievable distances. Some small. Some large. They glitter and they glisten. The silver orb of the moon, shines, moving in the heavens guided by God's hand. Sometimes it is only a half-moon. David said:

> *"When I consider the stars, when I consider the moon. When I consider the heavens, I know that thou has ordained it all by your wonderful fingers. Then he said, What is man? When I consider all of this. What is man that thou art mindful of him, And the son of man that thou visiteth him" (paraphrase Psalm 8:3-9).*

God is mindful of you because you are His masterpiece.

Did you know that God will come to you and visit you? "God, who made the heavens, will come and visit me?" you question. God, who made the moon, will come and visit you and me? God, who is mindful of every star, having even named every star, will come and visit with you and me? Yes. Yes! He will!

David goes on to say, *"Thou madest him to have dominion over the works of Thy hands. Thou hast put all things under his feet" (Psalm 8:6).*

What a privilege! What an honor to know that God has given us dominion. Why? Because He made us in His likeness. He made you and me like Him. He made you and me in the image of God.

Don't feel defeated. Don't be dismayed. You are God's masterpiece.

FATHER, SON AND THE HOLY SPIRIT (In Type)

"And it came to pass after these things, that God did tempt Abraham, and said unto him, Abraham; and he said behold, here I am. And he said, Take now thy son, thine only son Isaac, whom thou lovest, and get thee into the land of Moriah; and offer him there for a burnt offering upon one of the mountains which I will tell thee of. And Abraham rose up early in the morning, and saddled his ass, and took two of his young men with him, and Isaac his son, and clave the wood for the burnt offering, and rose up, and went unto the place of which God had told him. Then on the third day Abraham lifted up his eyes, and saw the place afar off. And Abraham said unto his young servant, Abide ye here with the ass; and I and the lad will go yonder and worship, and come again to you" (*Genesis 22:1-11*).

ABRAHAM

God selected a people through Abraham's descendants who would carry out His promise of redemption. God, the Father, God, the Son (Jesus Christ), the soon coming Son of God — Jesus Christ, and the Holy Spirit are a picture of the Holy Trinity as shown in the Book of Genesis. God's far reaching plan always reveals the blessed Son Jesus, in all His various godly attributes throughout the entire *Bible.*

Every aspect of creation, the universe, the moon and stars, the sun, the beasts, man and nature, both spiritually and physically, give us a picture of the Savior of the world. Through Abraham and Isaac we are again shown the Father and Son in type.

Early in the Book of Genesis, the great faith and obedience of Abraham is evident as he attests to the young men, *"I and the lad will go yonder and worship, and come again to you" (Genesis 22:5).*

"And Abraham took the wood of the burnt offering, and laid it upon Isaac his son; and he took the fire in his hand, and a knife; and they went both of them together" (Genesis 22:6).

And Isaac spake unto Abraham his father, and said, *"My father..."*

And he (Abraham) said, "*Here am I, my son."*

And he (Isaac) said, *"Behold the fire and the wood; but where is the lamb for a burnt offering"(Genesis 22:7)?*

Here we see Abraham, an earthly father, preparing his son to be a sacrifice. As God in heaven prepared his Son Jesus as a sacrifice for us:

> *And they came to the place which God built an altar there, and laid the wood in order, and bound Isaac his son, and laid him on the altar upon the wood. And Abraham stretched forth his hand, and took the knife to slay his son. And the angel of the Lord called unto him out of heaven, and said, "Abraham, Abraham" and he said "Here I am."*
>
> *And he said, "Lay not thine hand upon the lad, neither do thou anything unto him: for now I know that thou fearest God, seeing thou hast not withheld thy son, thine only son from me" (Genesis 22:9-12).*

God's mercy is shown again in saving Isaac from sacrificial slaughter. At the same time, God knew only man, who was both God and man, could ever shed His blood sacrificially.

Additionally, we see God is able to speak to us out of heaven, and that He honors and rewards our obedience by canceling our debt to Him. Christ Jesus would pay the debt in time to come.

ISAAC

We see Isaac as the perfect type of Jesus. Isaac, like Jesus, had been offered up for sacrifice.

Matthew 27 gives us a comparison. We see Isaac's meekness, his obedience and his willingness to obey his father, for Isaac was bound, and there is no record of any resistance to what his father had to do. There is no record that he tried to get off the altar.

It was a very tense moment as the knife was raised. Just imagine this. A child (Isaac) is lying on the altar watching his father raise a knife to slay him. Yet, Isaac remained silent on the altar. Isaac could have wrestled the knife from his father's hand, or just refused to lay upon the altar, period.

But, like Jesus, who did not raise a hand against those who would slay him, although He could have called legions of angels to rescue him, so Isaac did not raise a hand to save himself.

Jesus was also tempted by the Roman soldiers to save Himself if he were truly God, but He went to the cross in total obedience to His Father, even unto death.

Philippians 2:6-8 speaks of Jesus' humility and obedience:

> *Who, being in the form of God, thought it not robbery to be equal with God: But made himself of no reputation, and took upon him the form of a servant, and was made in the likeness of men; and being found in fashion as a man, he humbled himself, and became obedient unto death, even the death on the cross.*

So, Isaac was a type of Christ.

I wonder how many Christians have been obedient and put their flesh upon the altar as Isaac was laid upon the altar. Jesus died for man. Man must die for Him.

Isaac was bound by a cord, but Christians today are bound by the Covenant of Abraham, God's promises. But like Abraham and Isaac, to receive the covering of the covenant given to Abraham, to receive God's prosperity in all our ways, we must be obedient, even unto death if need be. As God gave a kingdom to Abraham through obedience, we can only inherit the Kingdom of God by obedience.

Paul tells us that, "*He that spared not His own Son, but delivered him up for us all, how shall he not with him also freely give us all things"(Romans 8:32)?*

Because of Isaac's obedience, being a type of Jesus, God honored His promise— His covenant with Abraham. Abraham was blessed, and Isaac was blessed. Through Christ Jesus, His Son, God gave us all things.

HOLY SPIRIT

What of the Holy Spirit? Are we given a type of the sweet Holy Spirit?

Genesis 24 tells us Abraham sends Eliezer for a bride for Isaac. Eliezer is of a type of the Holy Spirit. Eliezer is a meek servant; he is obedient, like the Holy Spirit.

Eliezer's only concern was to comply with his master's wish, never a thought for himself. Had Isaac not been born, Eliezer would have been the heir.

Eliezer started out in obedience of his master to look for a bride for Isaac. His meeting Rebekah at the well seems coincidental, but God was directing Eliezer's steps. Arriving at the well to water his animals, he met Rebekah. He was concerned, however, that she would not want to come with him and return as a bride for Isaac. But God had already gone before him to prepare the bride for Isaac. Eliezer prayed for his master and for favor with the woman. He had one thought in mind, to obey the master's plan.

All went as God had planned at the well, and Rebekah invited Eliezer to come home with her to meet her father. After meeting Rebekah's father, a contract was agreed upon by the father and Eliezer. Then, Eliezer began to give the gifts sent to Rebekah by his master.

Likewise, when a person decides to receive Christ as Lord, it's the same as making a contract with God that we want to become His child, and then the Holy Spirit takes the things of God and gives them to the church, just as Eliezer took the things of the bridegroom for the bride. Eliezer never spoke of himself, but only the things of the master. Jesus is the bridegroom and we are the bride. The Holy Spirit speaks of the things of God.

Jesus said of the Holy Spirit, *"He shall glorify me; for he shall receive of mine and shew it unto you" (John 16:14).*

For a more complete study on the Holy Spirit and what Jesus says He will do, read all of Chapter 16 of the Gospel of John.

RESURRECTION LIFE

"That I may know him, and the power of his Resurrection" (Philippians 3:10).

I have lived by, walked by and preached Philippians 3:10. What power did Jesus have when he came out of the tomb? This great event which affects us as a child of God is explained by Paul:

> *Therefore we are buried with him by baptism into death; that like as Christ was raised up from the dead by the glory of the Father, even so we also should walk in newness of life. For if we have been planted together in the likeness of his death, we share also in the likeness of his resurrection (Romans 6:4-5).*

The power of the resurrection brings a new spirit. The Scripture says we "should" walk in newness. The old carnal spirit, the doubt, the unbelief, and the impossible have died, never to be raised in us again.

The resurrection brought forth more than a physical body. It brought us into identification with Jesus. We can stop struggling with the old, sinful life. Jesus has set us free. We now walk in a new realm, possessing power with God, a divine power.

I prayed this prayer for years; it was not made real to me until after Rickey's death. The Lord spoke to me one day and said "Loretta, there wasn't resurrection, until after death."

The scripture confirms our new walk in God:

> *For in that he died, he died unto sin once, but in that he liveth, he liveth unto God. Likewise, reckon you also yourselves to be dead indeed unto sin, but alive unto God through Jesus Christ our Lord. Let not sin*

> *therefore reign in your mortal body, that ye should obey it in the lusts thereof. Neither yield ye your members as instruments of unrighteousness unto sin, yield yourselves unto God, as those that are alive from the dead, and your members as instruments of righteousness unto God (Romans 6:10-13).*

Resurrection power is a mighty strength. Resurrection life is not only that which raised Jesus from the dead. It is not only that which will raise the dead saints, but it brings power to overcome sickness, disease, poverty, and to conquer the enemy — both flesh and spirit.

You must read the Scriptures to know this power. Jesus said, *"Ye do err not knowing the scriptures, nor the power of God" (Matthew 22:29).*

St. Matthew emphatically states, *"I am the God of Abraham, and the God of Isaac, and the God of Jacob? God is not the God of the dead, but of the living"* (Matthew 22:32).

And like the Sadducees, the multitudes today who hear these words are astonished at His doctrine. But Jesus taught the power of the resurrection and had not yet experienced it! That is faith!

Do you have faith like Jesus? Although you are alive today, Jesus will raise you from the dead unto eternal glory. Can you believe God to catch up those who remain alive to meet Jesus in the air? Jesus believed before the fact, can you? The message is repeated a second time in Mark 12:24-28.

Can we walk in resurrection power though we yet live? Yes. Jesus imparted all his powers to us, if we receive Jesus as our Savior, and believe His promise and the power of His resurrection. He endowed the disciples of old with his power saying they could do the things they saw Him do, and even greater things. We are disciples, if we follow and believe Christ. So turn your power on! Believe and pray. Declare to Satan and to your trials that you live in resurrection life!

His resurrection power doesn't stop here. He delivered us from carrying grief. He bore our grief, carried our sorrows, our afflictions, our transgressions, our iniquities, and our sadness. As he arose that Easter morning with power, so shall we, when we are born again and do not err in knowing the promise of the scriptures.

Our new identification with Jesus says we must bring to a dying world the message that Jesus lives. He is alive with healing power, resurrection life power.

"In righteousness shall thou be established, thou shalt be far from oppression; for thou shalt not fear: and from terror; for it shall not come near thee" (Isaiah 54:14).

Resurrection power destroys fear and oppression. It heals all. Jesus told me to go preach the gospel and teach the word, and these signs shall follow. Those of you, who have believed with me, loved me, and supported me have shared in my work for God.

In our crusades the resurrection power of God works. We see people healed of heart trouble, cancer, blood diseases, back trouble, leg trouble, and many other afflictions. Many confess belief in Jesus as their Savior and receive salvation and glorify God, knowing that they are now saved from eternity in the lake of fire.

I praise God for our partners sending me from city to city to take the resurrection power of God.

One lady asked, "Does this stuff work?"

I said, "What?"

She said, "This— what you are doing — praying."

I asked, "Are you a Christian?"

She replied, "No, I don't go to church. I don't know how I got here."

She was bent over like the woman in the *Bible.* I prayed for her. God touched her and then I led her to the Lord. She received two miracles, healing and salvation. Salvation is the greatest miracle bought by Jesus' death, His blood and resurrection power! Now, she knows.

In that same meeting, there were at least a dozen young people who came forth, saying they were going blind. I was amazed at the youth in that church. Satan had afflicted them with sickness.

I had met their pastor in Korea in 1989. He had begun a great work for God, but the enemy was afflicting his people. My heart was truly stirred. I wondered how many other churches were in this same condition; young people on fire for God and the enemy moving against them. I challenged their faith in God.

In another meeting, one lady hired a driver to bring her from Lancaster to the 10:00 a.m. meeting. Her shoulder had been badly hurt from a fall. God healed her.

After returning to Dallas, I was informed that a lady I had prayed for at Baylor Hospital had been healed of cancer and had been sent home.

I praise God for His Word. The Word of God is power to overcome all things, even death. You can quote the Word to defeat Satan.

Trust the Word. Hebrews 4:2 says: "*The Word preached did not profit them, not being mixed with faith in them that heard it.*"

The Word of God is proven in our crusades. I preach with faith, the people believe the Word, and God answers prayer.

By walking in faith, we are in complete obedience to God. We now discover He will indeed provide our needs, and answer our prayer. Faith moves the hand of God.

THE THREEFOLD PURPOSE OF JESUS

***"For God so loved the world, that he gave his only begotten son,that whosoever believeth in him should not perish, but have everlasting life"* (John 3:16).**

Jesus Is Manifested Love

The Word of God expresses throughout the *Bible* that God is love. The highest expression of love is told in the golden text of the *Bible,* John 3:16. One great purpose of Jesus was to manifest the love of God. I have always said, and will continue to say until Jesus takes me to heaven: For God so loved the world that He gave the thing most precious to Him, His only Son. That was love expressed.

I doubt that many Christians would give their child to die that someone else would live. Yet, that is what Father God did, He so loved the world He sent His Son to die for each one of us. He loves those who do not know Him; He loves them equally. He loved them so much He offered Jesus' life that they should not perish but have everlasting life.

For one moment, imagine what heaven must have been like without the presence of Jesus; how the Father must have watched Mary as she so tenderly cradled the Son of the Living God in her arms. God must have yearned for His Son to be back in heaven. Yet, when He looked at the world, He allowed Jesus to come, conceived by the Holy Spirit as a little baby, to pay the price for you to sit in heavenly places with Him.

Someone had to pay the price. The world doesn't know that Jesus has paid a price unless someone tells them. We must tell them Jesus came to manifest the love of God.

As a baby, Jesus was helpless. He no longer had the status that He had in Heaven. He was a little baby being entrusted to a woman to hold, to care for, to cuddle, and to feed. With all our shortcomings, God trusted humans to raise this blessed baby, the very son of God! He gave Him that all the world might know Him and have everlasting life.

When you think of what Jesus came to earth to do, it should make you say, "Lord, I give you all of me." What a price He paid. He came to manifest the love of God.

What is the love of God? God's love is sure. It is vital. It is unconditional. It is everlasting. Every person needs that kind of love. Everything revolves around love. It is compassion toward others. God's love is so great that when we ask for one measure, He will give us seven. If you love, you will give: you will give your heart, you will give your time, and you will give your life.

At the birth of Jesus, God manifested His love. Today, He still manifests His love. Tomorrow, He will manifest His love, and the next day, and the next day, until He takes us into eternity. Serving God is worth the price to receive God's eternal love. He gave in love that man should not perish, nor suffer defeat.

Jesus The Healer — Deliverer

The second purpose that Jesus came for was to do the work of God; what are the works of God? Look at John 9:1: "*And Jesus passed by and saw a man which was blind from his birth ...and his disciples asked him, Master, who did sin" (John 9:1)?*

It always amazes me how people think if one becomes sick, somebody sinned. The disciples asked**:** *"Who did sin, this man, or his parents, that he was born blind"(John 9:2)?*

Jesus answered: *"Neither has this man sinned nor his parents, that the works of God should be manifest in him" (John 9:3).*

I read about a man who was on the road to Damascus, an ordinary man. His name was Saul; he was persecuting the Christians. He journeyed toward Damascus when suddenly there shined round about him a light from heaven.

This man's life is a picture of a man we would consider beyond the reach of even God's hand, but there is not a sinner born who is too rough, too tough, or too far gone, whom God cannot manifest His works through, and change him.

Saul was on his way to persecute God's people when there came a bright light. The word of God said it came from heaven. Saul fell from his horse when he heard a voice**.**

God was speaking to him. When Saul fell to the ground, God said: *"Saul, Saul why persecutest thou me" (Acts 9:4)?*

If the church ever gets hold of this, we will stop persecuting each other. When you persecute someone who belongs to God, you are persecuting God.

Saul replied to the Lord's question*, "Who art thou, Lord?"*

"I am Jesus whom thou persecutest."

Remember the scripture where Jesus said:

Inasmuch as ye have done it unto one of the least of these, you have done it unto me (Matthew 25:40).

As Saul trembled in astonishment, he said**,** "*Lord, what will thou have me do?"*

The first thing Saul wanted to ask God at his first encounter was **"What do you want me to do?"**

This man had never heard a sermon; he knew the Law, but he didn't know God. Until this day he had never been in the presence of God. Yet we have a two-way conversation going. The Lord said unto him, *"Arise and go into the city and it shall be told thee what thou must do."*

The men who journeyed with him stood speechless. Imagine! They did not hear God's voice. This is because God speaks to us individually. God observes us individually, and loves us individually, even if we were the only individual on earth.

Saul rose from the ground and obeyed. His eyes were blinded by the brilliance of God's light. Saul's men led him and brought him to Damascus. He was there three days without sight, neither did he eat.

There was a certain man named Ananias to whom the Lord gave a vision. The Lord said to him, *"Arise and go into the street which is called Straight, and inquire into the house of Judas for the one called Saul of Tarsus for behold he prayeth" (Acts 9:11).*

Notice, from the moment he had an encounter with God, that he began to pray.

Sometimes I wake up at two or three o'clock in the morning and begin to pray and to tell the Lord how much I love Him; how much I need Him and appreciate Him being with me, holding me. I just tell God how much my heart longs for Him.

I have walked this street in Damascus called Straight. I've walked this street where Paul had the encounter with the Living God. There you feel so close to the Lord.

In the vision he saw a man named Ananias who would come and put his hands on him that he might receive his sight.

When God begins to move, He works on both ends of the line. God speaks to all concerned. He spoke to Saul. He spoke to Ananias and instructed him where to go and what he was to do. He always confirms His Word.

God told Saul a particular man, whose name he even called, was going to come and lay hands upon him that he would receive his sight. When God speaks the same thing, He said to you or someone else, you have confirmation that God was speaking to you. Saul was a changed man. Before an encounter with God, he persecuted more Christians than any other man. But when a man finds God and receives the heart changing power, a miracle occurs. The Lord said unto him, through Ananias, "*Go thy way for He is a chosen vessel unto me*" (Acts *9:15*).

As you read this devotional, you may begin to feel that you are a chosen vessel. Respond to The Holy Spirit prompting.

The third purpose of Jesus is to demonstrate the will of God: By His will, God calls out the chosen vessels. It is the will of God that Jesus came to do the work of God. God chose Saul by His will to do a work.

What was the work of God in the beginning? God spoke and said let there be light. And there was light. He said let there be.... And there was.

God, from the very beginning, was doing a work, but it didn't end at creation. There is work to be done today. Jesus came to do the works of God. He said, "*I must work the works of him that sent me" (John 9:4).*

The lepers that came to Him said, "If you will, you can heal us."

Jesus replied, "I will," and they were healed. Jesus was manifesting the works of God as he did when he anointed Ananias with His power to open Saul's blinded eye, eyes that previously looked upon God's people with malice and destruction. Maybe Saul was blinded so he would see men in a new light. When God opened Saul's eyes, he reached out for the Lord. The works of God were made manifest that day.

Another time a man came to Jesus with a withered hand. Jesus said, Stretch out your hand. In obedience he did, and he was healed. Jesus was manifesting the power of God.

Jesus said, *"My meat is to do the will of him that sent me" (John 4:34).*

You have, most likely, asked God what is His will for you. No doubt, Saul was on his way to throw a few more Christians in jail. His course was set that day. He must have sat tall on his horse, commanding the soldiers around him. He thought he knew his purpose, what the Will of God was for his life. But he didn't really know, until his encounter with God.

One day the disciples wanted Jesus to break bread and eat with them, but Jesus said, *"I must go and finish the work of my father while I can"(paraphrased John 4:34).*

God's will for Jesus to die on the cross was established before he was ever sent as a babe from heaven. God did not do this for Jesus. For Jesus was already in heaven with Him. Jesus already stood at the right hand of God. Jesus was sent to earth to do the will of the Father, and that will was to die on a cross that you and I might be saved. When Jesus died, He paid the supreme price for you and me that we may also work the works of God.

APPRECIATION

By Jack Maclean, Southport QLD

It was a privilege to be introduced to Loretta Blasingame by Sir Lionel Luckhoo in July, 1994 in California.

Subsequent to a review of Loretta's credentials – Faith Restoration International (registered in Wellington, New Zealand) – a charitable trust of which I was a trustee, made arrangements for Loretta to visit New Zealand in late 1994.

Loretta was accompanied by Laete Thomas and a week of daily teaching and evening public meetings were arranged. These meetings were well attended (recognizing New Zealand's numbers are less than what some may be accustomed to).

Loretta has been blessed with an anointed teaching gift and teaches the uncompromised Word of God. Her commitment to bring her messages back to the Word of God is to be promoted and encouraged.

Both during daytime and evening meetings, the Holy Spirit revealed His presence with miraculous healings and deliverance. Between meetings, Loretta willingly made herself available and offered godly counsel to a number of attendees requiring guidance. God used Loretta in a wonderful way in some difficult circumstances.

The body of Christ was greatly uplifted by her visit, lives were changed, healings occurred and God was glorified.

Should the reader wish to discuss the visit or Loretta's ministry further, please do not hesitate to direct inquiries to me.

APPRECIATION

By Dr. William L. Whitlow

It has been my privilege to know Loretta Blasingame for the last twenty years. During this time I have seen her ministering on several occasions in the church that I pastor as well as in conference rooms.

My wife and I have watched her minister and have stood with her during her recent serious illness. Her character is unwavering toward God.

In the hardest of times, she does not blame God, but resigns herself that whatever this trial is about, she will go through it with her wonderful Jesus and for His gain in her life.

Loretta reminds me not of one, but two ladies in the scripture. They are "Mary the Devotee" and "Martha the Servant".

Mary demonstrated three actions which I see in Loretta:

1. The action of devotion. She is a HEARER—"Mary who also sat at Jesus' feet and heard His word" and "Mary has chose that good part." (Luke 10:39, 41)

2. The action of identification, she is a GIVER—"It was Mary who anointed the Lord with fragrant oil and wiped his feet with her hair." (James 11:2)

3. The action of lamentation, she is an AGONIZER—"Let her along. Why do you trouble her? She has done a good work for me. She had done what she could." (Mark 14:6,8a)

These three actions are demonstrated in her life. She has been in the presence of Jesus in Heaven and waits before Him at His feet in the study of the Word to hear His voice.

As she daily anoints the feet of Jesus with her tears, seeking Him to perfect her life before Him in ministry, she agonizes hour after hour in prayer for the saved to be converted to Christ in her meetings and be healed.

Martha also demonstrates three functions which I see in Loretta: (Luke 10:38-42)

1. The function of HOSPITALITY—"Martha welcomed (Jesus) into her house. (vs.38) She lives for the presence of Jesus. Having had a personal tour about heaven as He held her arm, she spends hours before Him. This hospitality also reaches out beyond her home to others, ministers and laity that need her comfort and counsel.

2. The function of RESPONSIBILITY—"Lord, do you not care that my sister has left me to serve alone?" (vs. 40) Loretta does serve as a single person and the load gets heavy so she needs our help to lift the load. No doubt there are times when she cried out, "Lord, tell someone to help me."

3. The function of ACCOUNTABILITY—"Lord, if you had been here, my brother would not have died."

Martha demonstrates these areas of faith.

1. "Healing" faith (vs.21)—Loretta's ministry demonstrates her healing faith all over the world.

2. "Creating" faith (vs. 22)—"I hear that whatever you ask of God, God will give you." Loretta is not only seeing miracles, but recreative miracles are happening in her meetings.

3. "Redeeming" faith (vs. 27)—"Yes. Lord, I believe that you are the Christ, the Son of God."

Loretta's main objective is bringing souls to Christ. She has a good balanced presentation of professional music, the preached Word, and the prayer of faith for healing and miracles.

I do believe that God has raised her up for an effective ministry in these closing days of time. John 11:5 states: "Now Jesus loved Martha and her sisters"—I am convinced that Jesus loves the "Mary-devotee" quality and the "Martha-servant" quality in Loretta. These combine into the Loretta Blasingame Ministries. To God is the Glory!

Crusade Attire

Loretta Blasingame when she ministered in Los Angeles in the mid 1980's and also at Melodyland Christian Center for Dr. Ralph Wilkerson in Anaheim, CA.

Early Days of Ministry

Full Gospel Central Church is the largest church in the world. Pastored by Dr. David Yonggi Cho.

Loretta was privileged to personally meet Dr. David Yongi Cho in 1989.

She was given a word from the Lord concerning her being a woman of prayer and faith.

International Ministry

NEW ZEALAND

Loretta Blasingame held a Healing Crusade in the Christian Revival Centre in New Zealand, on August 24, 1994, the same church where Smith Wigglesworth began his global ministry 78 years earlier.

Loretta on the platform in The Christian Revival Centre.

*Pictured: Josh Maclean (second from left,
Sister Laete Thomas (middle) and the sponsoring family
of Loretta Blasingame's Crusade.*

GRAND CAYMAN

Overflow crowd fills the hall in Grand Cayman

Picture - THE CAYMANIAN COMPASS – November 19, 1993

Great miracles took place in Loretta's Grand Cayman Crusade

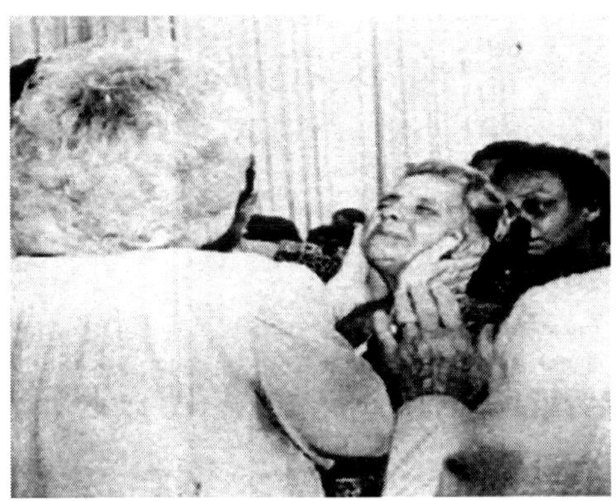

Picture - THE CAYMANIAN COMPASS – November 19, 1993

Loretta Blasingame was blessed to Co-coordinate Evander and Dr. Janice Holyfield's Holy Warriors Ministry, Las Vegas, NV Crusade.

Dr. Janice Holyfield is an outstanding minister and a great woman of God. Evander is the Three-time World Heavyweight Boxing Champion of the World.

Loretta while awaiting a Trinity Broadcasting (TBN) taping in Irving, TX

Special Friendships Over The Years

Loretta with close friends Dr. J. C. and Virginia Fikes. Loretta started her first church in their home in CA. They call her their "adopted daughter".

Loretta and close friends Geri Turnbull (left) and Larry Chupp after ministering at North Coast United Methodist Church in Oceanside, CA.

Loretta with Evy, in her 80's who was dying in a Minnesota hospital. Loretta prayed for her and she has been out playing the piano ever since then. Evy recently cut her first CD.

Loretta and minister friends from Minnesota. Pictured left to right are: Rev. Phil Shaw and wife Faith, Pastors of New Life Church in Rochester, MN, and Evangelists Jonathan and Faye Reine.

Bishop, Dr. Francis Jackson – Pastors

Mt. Zion Church, one of the largest churches In Bangalore, India.

Reverend Peter Paul (Brother of Bishop Jackson)

Pastors The Rose Of Sharon Church in Augusta, GA.

Loretta ministers to Freda Lindsay, Founder of Christ For The Nations Institute in Dallas, TX. Loretta admires Sister Lindsay as one of the world's greatest women of faith.

Omagene Haft - Longtime friend, Spiritual Mother, Intercessor and supporter of Loretta's Ministry.

Dr. Loretta Blasingame with one of her dearest and closest friends, Dorothy Kennemer. Dorothy was healed under her ministry and became a great Intercessor and financial supporter for many years. At Dorothy's request, Loretta conducted her homegoing service when she was promoted to heaven in her nineties.

Contact The Author

Dr. Loretta Blasingame

Loretta Blasingame Ministries, Inc.

P. O. Box 4058

Fullerton, CA 92834-4058

(760) 593-0410

Please contact Dr. Blasingame to share how her book has encouraged your life. Your prayer requests are welcome.

For Media Sponsoring • Speaking Engagements • Crusade Information

Loretta Blasingame Ministries, Inc.

Attn: Events Department

P. O. Box 4058

Fullerton, CA 92834-4058

lblasingamemin@aol.com

www.pastorlbm.org

PRODUCTS

Order thru Website: www.pastorlbm.org OR Mail Check/Money Order with form to:

Loretta Blasingame Ministries, Inc.
Attn: Order Fullfillment Department
P. O. Box 4058
Fullerton, CA 92834-4058

Book - Is Anybody Up There?

_______ Softcover $14.95

_______ Hardcover $19.95

DVD - $7 each

_______ Testimony of "Little Joey" (5 min.)

Video - $7 each

_______ Testimony of "Little Joey" (5 min.)

_______ **Subtotal**

_______ **Please add $3 Shipping & Handling (US Post Office)**

_______ **Total Amount**

Ck#_______________ Money Order #______________________________

Name____

Address____

City________________________ State_______ Zip__________-________

Phone ( ) __________ - ______________

Email____

(Please remove this page and mail with payment.)